Julian, Special Son.

OK, so you are Not Two pensioners, YET!
But I like the write-up on the back cover......
"It is also a tale of life's many adventures, and provides valuable lessons on pushing the bounds, keeping going when things don't go right" etc. All of which you both have in spades, even before you became pensioners!

Hope you enjoy this, which may not be a book you would know about, or would necessarily choose for yourself. It reminds me, in a limited way, of the satisfaction I had, over twelve months restoring Daphne.

With our love
Dad and Pat xxx

christmas 2020.

Seawater and Sawdust

Seawater and Sawdust

Two pensioners build a wooden boat

Tom & Lorraine Owen

SELF

PUBLISHING
HOUSE

Published in 2020 by Tom & Lorraine Owen
seawaterandsawdust@gmail.com

The information provided within this publication is for general informational and inspirational purposes only. It is sold on the understanding that the author and publisher are not engaged in rendering professional services. If professional advice or other expert assistance is required, the services of a competent professional should be sought. The author and publisher accept no responsibility for any errors or omissions, or for any accidents or mishaps that may arise from from the use of this publication.

Publishing services provided by Self Publishing House

Photographs © Lorraine Owen
except p1, p156–159 © Motor Boat and Yachting, used with permission

Sketches © Tom Owen

Hardback ISBN   978–1–9163873–3–1
Paperback ISBN 978–1–9163873–5–5
eBook ISBN   978–1–9163873–4–8

Two pensioners want a new wooden boat… so they build one

Contents

Introduction

My name is Lorraine Owen, and my husband Tom and I have built three boats together in the thirty-seven years of our marriage. This book is the story of the build of *Thea*, a project undertaken in our retirement and probably our last creation.

So, who are we? Tom has been involved in boatbuilding since the age of fourteen. He is entirely self-taught as vocational education didn't really exist when he was at school and there was little available in the way of marine apprenticeships. However, he could read and read he did, avidly working his way through a succession of 'how-to' books covering woodworking, boat design and construction, and engineering. His first practical project, still at the age of fourteen, was to design and build an 8-foot punt and everything had to be done on a shoestring as he was still at school. That was the beginning of a passion for boats and boating, and his life thereafter would always revolve around seawater and sawdust. His existence as a waterborne hippie altered a bit (the hair had to go) when he met me in 1981.

My life had been a lot more conservative – grammar school followed by the public sector. I had very little experience of doing anything practical, maybe the odd art class and some lacklustre gardening, but mainly my time had been spent socialising with my friends and having fun. I had spent my late teens working in the Home Office in London, and afterwork parties were the name of the game.

With our disparate backgrounds, the odds of us meeting were extremely long. Tom and I had both moved down to Devon in 1976, Tom on the boat he

Him and Me

then had and me following my parents who chose to retire there. I worked in the local Further Education College in Torquay, who funded termly 'socials' for the lucrative 'English as a Foreign Language' market, to which young college staff, midshipmen from Dartmouth Naval College and junior doctors and nurses from the local hospital were invited. They were fun events and a great place to meet people. Previously at these jamborees I had met and then dated naval officers, teachers and other professionals. At the Christmas 1981 event, when we were in our late twenties, Tom was dragged along by a College librarian and her husband, who had offered him a room in their house to save him from freezing to death in the derelict caravan he had been living in. It was the original 'eyes met across a crowded room' and the rest, as they say, is history. Neither of us had been looking for a permanent relationship, never mind marriage, but for both of us it was a Thumper from *Bambi* moment. We moved into a dilapidated stone cottage on our wedding day and we still live there today. We've always been too busy with one project or another to think of moving.

When I met Tom he had an Elizabethan 33, *Souena*, which he had fitted out from a hull and deck moulding. I had never been on a small boat before. My family are 'Navy' and I'd spent enough time on ships and ferries to know that I would never be seasick. If I should have had any qualms about adding 'boating' to my list of hobbies I was too young and in love to be aware of them. As it happened, I took to the whole thing like a duck to water. We had three very happy summers spending our holidays on board and cruising the southwest coast getting wet and cold in equal quantities; *Souena* threw water over anyone and everyone in the cockpit. I distinctly remember apologising profusely to a dear friend as many gallons of saltwater burst over the decks and unerringly poured down the neck of his oilskins.

In 1983, when we got married and took on the cottage, the mortgage rate was running at 14% and, as time went on, it became obvious that my salary and Tom's self-employed income weren't enough to cover our mortgage, run *Souena* and restore the derelict property that we were living in. We had to live upstairs for three years, with no hot water, no kitchen and not

Souena on her mooring in the River Dart

much of a bathroom. Life was a bit of a trial. We were just treading water with no money to do anything other than survive. The sensible thing to do, which we ended up doing, was to sell *Souena* and pay off the mortgage. Selling something that you have created is always a painful thing to do but, as it turned out, losing the constant drain of the mortgage gave us the freedom to spend a lifetime building and enjoying a series of boats.

Tom was like a man with no arms when he had no boat in his life. I was earning a reasonable salary by this time and I couldn't and wouldn't squash his need to create. I loved my job and was happy to give him the freedom to start a new project. Our first boat build together was in 1990 when we were in our thirties – a 22-foot angling boat made of glass fibre. Tom took me down to a scrappy old boatyard in Southampton and we found a heap of planks loosely held together in the shape of a motorboat. It was cheap and all we could afford so we bought it and had it transported back to Devon. Tom got the hulk stable enough to use as a plug, upon which we created a mould. Finally, we laid up the first hull, which, astonishingly, came out of the mould without too much trauma. We were thinking that we could go into production but unfortunately the whole experience was entirely unpleasant – sticky, smelly and itchy. I worked in an office during the day and then came down to the yard every evening and weekend. The glass fibre work was horrendous and broke my childhood dream. One of my heroines had been Emma Peel in *The Avengers*, who wore catsuits and knee-high boots. Instead of the sultry catsuit I had dreamed of, I was wearing a disgusting one-piece overall, covered in resin and strands of fibreglass. Instead of the knee-high black leather boots, I wrapped my feet and legs in clingfilm to avoid sticking to the hull. But we persevered and completed the fit-out of the hull, calling the boat *Early Mist*. We had already decided that GRP boat production was something that neither of us enjoyed and certainly didn't

Early Mist - River Lynher, Plymouth

want to repeat. But *Early Mist* was a pretty little thing and we loved her, spending a couple of happy years cruising the southwest coast for our holidays, and going fishing most nights after work. We sold the moulds and, as far as we know, they ended up in Scotland. Maybe they are still producing hulls!

Although we were happy with *Early Mist*, some friends took

us out on their yacht in Plymouth Sound. We heard the 'tick tick' sound of a strong wind stretching the sheets and piling on the power and we realised that we hadn't finished with the joys of fighting the helm and being soaked. So, "Let's build a boat," Tom said to me in 1993 when we were in our early forties. (Not a strange thing for a boat builder to say, and something I'd heard before and would hear again…) Warming to his theme now, he continued: "We can use our nearby boatyard on the River Dart, and we are still fit, strong and healthy," – he didn't add "and possibly stupid".

We considered buying a 'Tradewind 35' GRP hull and fitting it out, but the price of the hull and deck mouldings would have taken too much of our budget. Anyway, Tom had the skills to design and build a wooden boat from scratch and, of course, that was what he really wanted to do. Fortunately, by this time he was able to take a couple of years' break from paid work, so we decided to go for it. Settling on a combination of modern and traditional construction methods, we used timber and epoxy resin to lay up the hull with triple diagonal iroko planking, choosing a composite deck using tongue and groove, and marine ply. One of the advantages of this was that Tom could do most of the labour himself without my help – I had to stay employed to earn the money to pay for the build, and to pay for us to maintain our house and lifestyle. We quickly realised that using timber and epoxy was an excellent build method – to our mind infinitely preferable to working with GRP.

Life wasn't exactly a breeze for me, though, working full time and then putting in every evening and weekend in the large plastic tent that we built as our workshop. I would cook our supper, put it in Tupperware boxes, and take it to the shed so we could work through the evening. We made the mistake of accepting the gift of an old settee and the comfort of this disrupted progress a bit. We were so tired we'd just fall asleep after tea. Visiting friends would creep away without disturbing us, saying we looked like Babes in the Wood, sleeping amongst the sawdust.

The shed was like a greenhouse – cold and damp with condensation in the winter, and blisteringly hot in the summer. Of course, Tom had to put up with that all the time – at least I had a comfortable office to lurk in during the day. We survived and after two and a half years we had our beautiful yacht *Selene*.

Selene - Sneem Harbour, County Kerry, Ireland

She was our pride and joy, and we sailed her for over twenty years, covering 12,500 miles.

As we both approached our sixties, we realised that maybe something needed to change. We were both finding that being wet, cold and sometimes frightened out in an open cockpit was no longer as appealing as it had been. Also, *Selene* had clocked up many miles and we had done pretty much everything we were ever going to do in a sailboat with our preferred cruising ground restrictions. Blue water sailing had never been our intention – we like the excitement of the arrival and departure and not really extended time at sea. We like to explore creeks and estuaries, getting involved with fellow sailors and local communities. We had become slightly dissatisfied with our cruising life and needed a new direction.

Tom is an 'ideas' man and is constantly thinking about prospective boat designs so he spent a couple of years tossing things around in his mind and on a drawing board. It came as no surprise to me in 2015 when he said, "Let's build a boat." After all, I'd heard it before, twice! But I can't say I was overly enthusiastic – I'd done it before, twice! With a combined age of one hundred and twenty-seven, another session in a boat shed wasn't high on my to-do list. I knew he'd spent furtive hours at his drawing board up in his studio, but I'd hoped it was just one of those 'man' things, something he'd lose interest in when the spring came. "No," I whimpered, "I don't want to spend every day in manky overalls looking like a chicken shed floor again. I don't want to miss fun times out with my friends because we've got some time deadline with paint systems or resin curing. I want to have manicures, pedicures, unsuitable streaks, painful toning sessions, all the things that women of my age are meant to do. I want to drink copious amounts of wine and worry about liver function tests. I don't want to build another boat!"

But Tom is a life-long boat designer and builder and he was convinced that we had one more boat in us. Optimism and passion outvoted sloth and memories of backbreaking work, and another dream started to become a reality. Twenty months later we had our lovely 30-foot motorboat *Thea*, named after the Greek goddess of the shining light of the clear blue sky, and a defender of sailors.

And this book is her story.

And suddenly you know:
It's time to start something new and trust the magic of beginnings.

–Meister Eckhart

Decisions, decisions

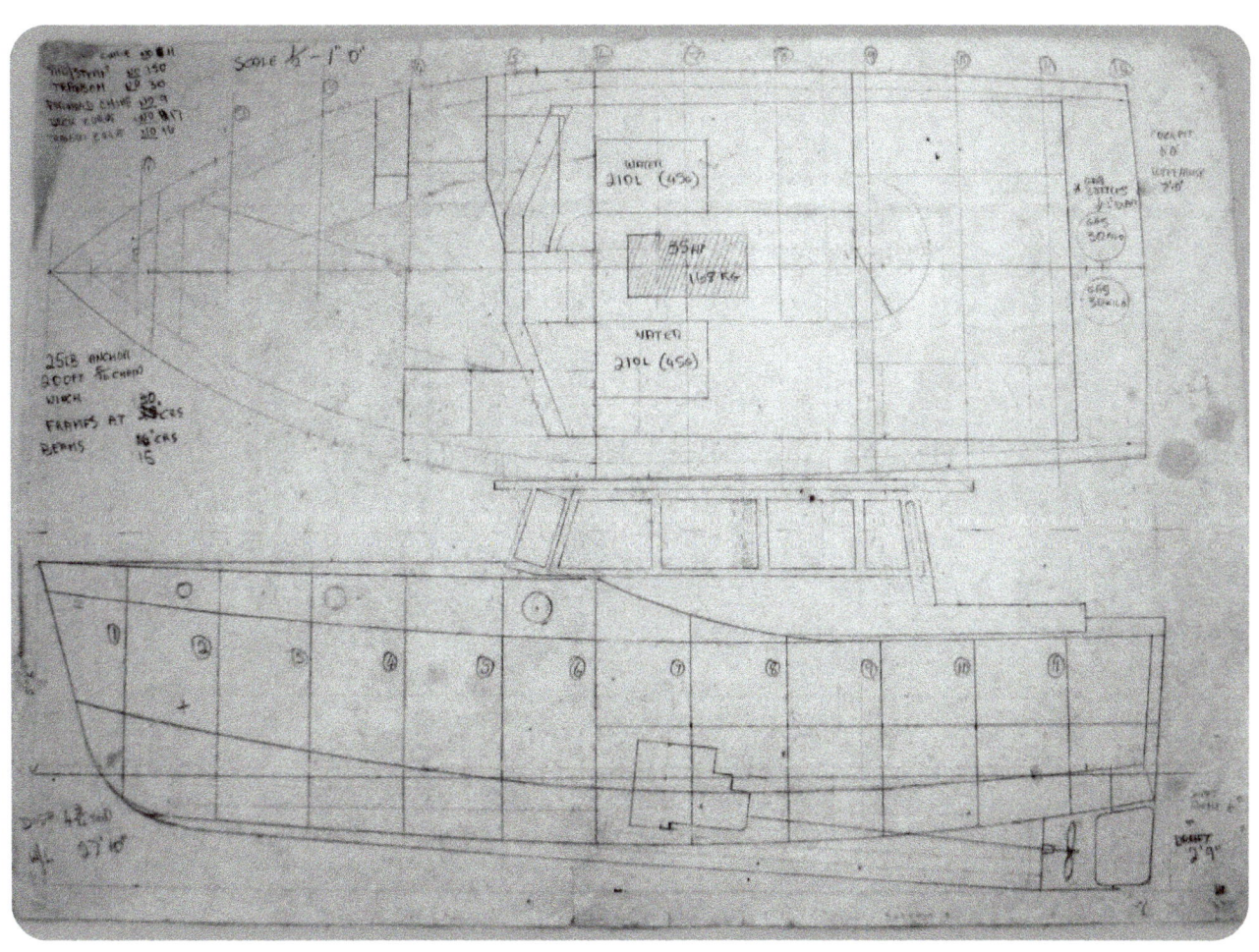

Thea's study plan

In which…
- We decide what to do
- We decide how to do it

2015-2016
LAUNCH DAY MINUS
TWO YEARS

Sail to Motor

Having owned up to each other that we are a bit fed up with being damp and cold, it becomes obvious that we might be ready to go over to the 'dark side' and consider a motorboat, after all we had had really good times on *Early Mist*. We don't enjoy spending long hours beating to windward when the same journey can be achieved in a fraction of the time under motor. Perhaps it is just our bad luck, but our travels on yachts all too often seem to be into the wind, and our logs show that we have our engine on for seventy percent of the time. With this as a yardstick it doesn't seem unreasonable to have our engine on one hundred percent of the time, driving a hull designed to be propelled by motor. With our advancing age we realise that we are more likely to be able to use a motorboat into our dotage, avoiding the much more strenuous effort involved with a yacht.

The germ of an idea for a motorboat had already taken shape in Tom's mind and he had played around on his drawing board for a couple of years while we wrestled with the decision about whether to move on from our much-loved *Selene*. Tom has the capacity to visualise plans as they will appear in three dimensions. I don't, and over the winter Tom made a small-scale model to let me see what he has in mind. It's delightful and is a great help to me to gain confidence in the project.

Eventually we decide to take the plunge. I know that Tom is desperate to build the new boat and if we don't hurry up and get on with it, we'll be too old to take on a project of this size.

Design

After a great deal of thought on Tom's part, and considerable debate and head scratching, we decide on the following specifications:

Length	30 ft
Beam	11 ft
Draft	3 ft
Displacement	4.75 tons

The Model

Designing the boat ourselves means that we can accommodate all the factors that are important to us and, with our previous experience of extended living aboard, we can design the accommodation to suit our needs exactly. For example:

Keeping costs down

- We expect the sale of *Selene* will generate enough to cover the building costs almost exactly, with nothing to spare. We have already retired so we will have to keep within our budget, and the finished boat will have to be economical to run. Keeping the size to 30 feet will mean that our mooring costs will be reasonable, i.e. expensive rather than extortionate.

- Having a relatively small engine will keep our fuel bills within sense and reason. We calculate that a 35hp diesel engine with a 215-litre (42-gallon) tank will give us a 450-mile cruising range at 6–7 knots. A single engine with a single shaft-driven screw will keep the machinery costs down. We finally decide on the Beta 35hp diesel.

Maximising comfort

- In particular, we want to have an enclosed wheelhouse, combining a comfortable lounge/dinette with a helm/navigation area. All of this 'living' space will have a 360-degree view of the world outside, something we've never had on our sailboats and which we covet. For the helm position, we plan to use a seat from a VW van, as it will be really comfortable and will give us multiple adjustment options, ensuring that whoever is at the helm can take advantage of the excellent visibility.

- We will buy a large 250 watt solar panel which should supply all of our reasonably modest electrical needs without having to run the main engine as a generator. The panel will be mounted safely out of the way and in full light/sun on the wheelhouse roof.

- We plan to paint our hull dark blue, as we did with *Selene*. We have found that this attracts the heat and promotes ventilation, keeping the boat dry and mould-free.

- We expect to limit the amount of roll because of the chine hull. We know all about rolling about inside our skins!

Fit for purpose

- I love to cook and insist on a good size galley and, being a creature of comfort in that direction, I also want a spacious heads.

- Tom has decided to have a raised foredeck area, which will provide good buoyancy in a seaway. This will maximise the internal space available and give standing headroom in the galley/heads area.

- The cockpit needs to be large enough to allow for fishing (another of Tom's passions) and to provide a sheltered outdoor lounging/alfresco dining area, but small enough to be safe on passage. Tom favours the traditional look, which will be visually timeless, but will incorporate the American idea of carrying a wide beam aft to provide stability and maximum capacity for length.

- We decide to fit davits on the stern deck, which will allow us to carry our solid dinghy safely out of the water on passage.

- Tom draws in a long keel to aid tracking and provide protection for the propeller. This is augmented by bilge keels to allow us to dry out, albeit at an angle. The size of these is sufficient for that purpose but not large enough to interfere unduly with water flow under the hull.

- The plans include high-volume water tanks for cruising, reducing the need to make water collection a regular occurrence. We tend to travel from anchorage to anchorage rather than marina to marina, so water is collected in jerrycans using the dinghy. If the weather is foul and the landing precarious, this can be more of a pain than a pleasure. Our capacity will be such that we can use water fairly generously, and only have to top up every month or so.

- Tom allows plenty of lockers for stowage. We will be stowing all of our personal kit in the main accommodation and we don't want to be living in a jumble.

- The boat's gear, including a large supply of bottled gas (2 x 15 kilos) and petrol for the outboard, will be kept safely in the cockpit lockers, two of which will drain outboard to remove any fumes or spillage. We will be using approximately one 15-kilo bottle of gas every two months, and two bottles last us for our summer cruise. It is much cheaper to buy 15-kilo bottles than the smaller 'dumpy' ones and using small bottles would mean endless searching for top-up supplies during the summer. We would definitely prefer to avoid that.

Future proofing

- It takes me a little time to persuade Tom that now would be a good time to invest in a serious electric anchor winch. He has always been happy to use a heavy duty manual winch in the past but, again with an eye to the future and as we need to buy a new winch anyway, it makes sense to spend a few extra pounds now and get something that hopefully will last a long time.

Once the plans have been drawn, and calculations completed, I am keen to pass them by a naval architect. Tom is a gifted designer but has no RINA (Royal Institute of Naval Architects) qualification. The build will be a big investment in terms of time and money and so we take the plans to a naval architect and ask him for confirmation that the design is sound. That done, we can inform our surveyor and our insurance company that the plans have been approved.

Build method

Selene's timber/epoxy construction had proved to be a real success, and we decide to use that combination again for *Thea* but using plywood instead of solid timber. Rather than use the labour-intensive triple diagonal method, we have opted for a plywood chine build. This will be quicker and will give us slightly greater volume and increased stability. The thing to avoid is going to be a 'boxy' look but Tom adds curves to everything in sight, which give the hull considerable grace.

The chine design means that we can use marine ply and epoxy for our hull, which is a well-established method of construction. This will be complemented by a solid timber wheelhouse, which will be relatively easy to build from timber sections and, when varnished, will look good both from the outside and from within.

The classic problem with plywood, and indeed with wooden boats generally, is the ingress of water. With modern epoxies it is possible to seal everything inside and out and create what is effectively an inert core. Nothing absorbs water and nothing expands and contracts – job done.

Using epoxy will also enable us to laminate complicated curves like deck beams and bow sections. The finished laminated section will be potentially stronger than a beam or section cut from a solid piece of wood.

The build site and shed

From previous experience we know that we will have to build a large temporary shed for our project. Our calculation is that we are going to be spending about a year 'in build' and we will have to have a reasonably watertight and sheltered build environment. There are several boatyards on the Dart and we scout around to find the best fit for the job. The once famous Philips shipyard at Noss, at the time in receivership and half derelict, steps up to the mark. They open their arms to us, not only agreeing to the building of the shed and the boat, but also giving us help and encouragement throughout. The yard produced vessels of many shapes and sizes, including those for the Navy and Trinity House, totalling thousands of tons over a period of one hundred and forty-one years, despite being bombed during World War Two, when the workforce suffered a number of fatalities. During the build the ownership of the yard passes to Premier Marinas but the staff and new owners are still full of enthusiasm and support. This never changes throughout our project, for which we will be eternally grateful. Under Premier Marinas, the vision of the yard will move to the leisure industry and projects like ours will no longer be possible. With its rich heritage, we like the thought that *Thea* will be the last boat to be built there.

And so the build begins…

Here we go again

Deck beam former

MARCH 2015
LAUNCH DAY MINUS TWENTY-ONE MONTHS

We are very excited to be on the brink of our new project and, after three years of soul searching, we are sure we have made the right decision. But it is still a bitter, bitter pill to swallow when we sign the sale document for *Selene*. We have spent about two years making this decision, always teetering on the brink and then running back to give her hug and say: "we didn't mean it". She represents so much hard work, so much adventure, so much fear and so much joy. She will always be in our hearts.

But the money is now available to fund this new step in our lives and we start to spend.

We are going to need a large quantity of quality hardwoods and marine ply to complete the build and choose Robbins Timber in Bristol as our supplier. After a trip up to look at their woodyard, it is obvious that they are going to be the best choice. Robbins have many years of experience with marine timber and they also have the right commercial cutting tools to machine things to our specification. We would prefer to prepare the timber stock ourselves, but we don't have the machinery to do it. Generally, DIY equipment isn't man enough for such heavy work and there comes a time when you have to accept that it is sensible to pay someone else to do something for you. We are a bit shocked to learn how much the price of wood has rocketed in the twenty years since we built *Selene* but, then, hasn't everything. Robbins prove to be both efficient and reliable and we quickly develop a good rapport with their sales staff and delivery driver. It's always more pleasant to give money to people you like.

The first thing we need to do is start the lamination of the 11-foot mahogany deck beams. This is going to be a long old job and we need to start work on them now so that they will be ready to be fitted in a few weeks' time. Tom has to build a former, which will take two beams at a time, but we are going to need a total of twenty-two of them and each laminate will have to be left to 'cure' for forty-eight hours on the former before it can be released. We've found in the past that curved laminates can 'spring' back if the need for this curing time isn't observed. All this means that the whole process is going to take nearly a month of short laminating sessions, so we need to start now to get them all finished by the time we will need them. We are going to use the conservatory in our garden to do this particular job as we can go there in the evening to make beams after finishing the day's work on the main project, all the time trying to avoid including Buddy, our cat, as a furry lump within the laminates.

The next spend is an order with Southern Timber, a woodyard in nearby Ipplepen. We need rough sawn plank and utility plywood from them in order to build the shed framework, and then we order polythene sheet online for the cover.

   With the materials ordered we can start preparing for the shed build. Noss boatyard have offered us our choice of spots in the yard, and we finally plump for what appears to be a slightly raised dry site, sheltered by the embankment of the Dart Steam Railway. This consequently proves to be an error, mind you, as it floods on high spring tides and in the winter a lot of water drains down off the embankment, running gently through the shed. So much for climate control. While we are wandering round inspecting the hardcore of our new home a lorry arrives, as promised, from Southern Timber with a great pile of goodies for the shed build. The yard staff are kind enough to help to unload everything. They have a large forklift truck which speeds things up enormously, and then we beetle home to collect tools, breakfast and courage.

   The shed will consist of ten A-frames spaced to give us an overall length of 34 feet, a width of 20 feet and an overall height to the roof apex of 20 feet. We've built large sheds before and we know that the erection of the first two frames will be rather exciting as they are mostly unsupported. Individually the frames are delicate and very flexible, and only become structurally sound once connected by quite a lot of bracing.

   First things first, Tom cuts the planking to size for the ten A-frames of the main shed body. Next, we cut plywood 'gussets',

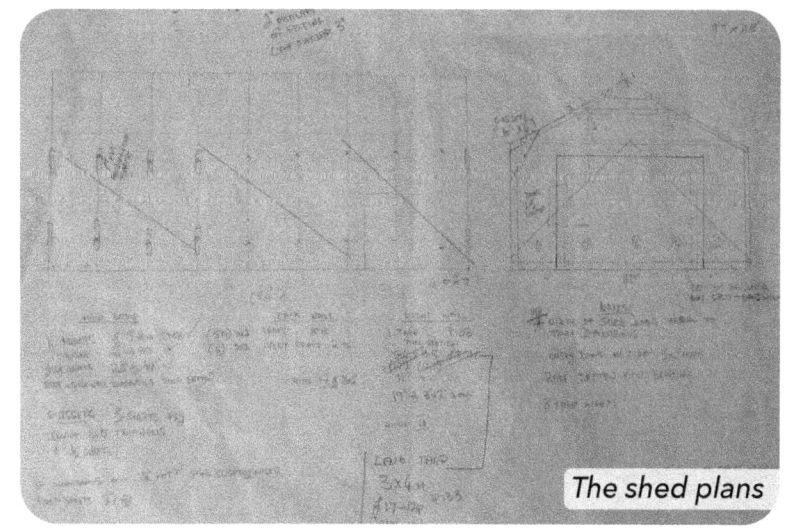

The shed plans

which are bolted to the ends of the plank sections to create the necessary angles of the A-frame. These will keep the frames solid and steady. There is a lot of head scratching while we calculate how to cut the maximum number of gussets from each sheet of plywood. The gussets are quite large and the calculation isn't easy, but eventually we manage to avoid too much wastage.

Once we've finished assembling the A-frames, we need to get them raised up. Our first attempt is predictably dismal. We can't keep the initial frame steady and we just can't remember how we did this last time (it was twenty plus years ago). Then I have the brilliant idea of looking at our photographs of the previous shed we built for *Selene*'s construction. We have forgotten

Assembling the frames

The first terrifying frames go up

that we used a scaffold tower – duh!!! A quick call to a tool hire firm and the next day a most welcome tower arrives, together with our long-suffering friends Michèle, Paul and Richard. Working as a team with several ropes being pulled in different directions is massively more effective than our feeble efforts with two ropes. As expected, the first two frames are still difficult but, once they are secure, they act as a gantry for everything else and within a couple of days we have the basic skeleton of a shed.

While all this has been going on, it's becoming apparent that all is not well with one of my hips. Climb-

Raising the shed frames - easy now with the scaffold

ing the scaffold is beyond me and even ladders are a bit of an issue. I'm a bit perplexed because I've always been reasonably fit and I don't carry excess weight, so I think I must have just 'pulled something'. My GP refers me for physio and some sessions in a local gym, but I'm really struggling. My brother takes me to task and tells me to pull my finger out and get myself referred to an orthopaedic specialist. I have an X-ray and see a consultant, and basically osteoarthritis is severe in my left hip joint and I'll have to have a replacement. The timing of this sucks. It wasn't part of our plan and to have surgery now will compromise our timetable significantly. We hope I will be able to muddle through by having steroid injections and wait until the end of the build to have the hip replaced. Meantime our friend Paul is helping with our ladder work. It isn't until later that we discover that (a) he hates heights and (b) his hip is also on the way out. What a way to treat your mates.

Now we have to cover the sides and top of the shed with polythene sheet. The first job is to find some unwanted carpet so that we can cut strips to pad all the edges of the frameworks. This provides protection for the polythene, avoiding chafe on the point of contact with the wood. Fortunately, Paul went to school with a chap who is now a carpet retailer and carpet offcuts duly arrive. The yard starts to echo with the sound of tacker guns attaching carpet strips to planking. We use the tacker guns with some care, still haunted by memories of Tom stapling his finger to the roof when we were building *Selene*'s shed.

Thinking back to our experience of *Selene*'s build, we remember the appalling heat that a polythene shed can generate. To try to mitigate this, we'll use standard polythene for the sides and ends but opaque heat reflective polythene to cover the roof. This is designed for polytunnels where it is used to protect delicate plants that can't take too much heat – a bit like us. Once again we gather our friends together and start the sweaty job of sliding many square metres of slippery sheet over something the size of a small house – without tearing the polythene – and soon we are weatherproof, apart from our 'ends'. Other friends have donated a lovely door and that soon becomes our entrance. With some thoughts of the winter to come, we decide that 'channels' dug into the hardcore just inside the sides of the shed might be useful to lead any rainwater away from our wood stores. This is a grizzly job but proves to be well worth the effort. On occasions the water runs along these channels swiftly enough to play pooh-sticks.

Another parcel of money leaves our coffers when we order the timber for the actual boat frames and the hull plywood. It will be a week or so before this all arrives, and we can give ourselves some time off to go to a couple of boat jumbles. This is part of our economy drive. There are zillions of bits and pieces to buy so anything saved is a bonus. Boat jumbles have saved us thousands of pounds over the years. Though as we embark on our money-saving jaunt, it becomes apparent that online discount chandleries are replacing the boat jumbles of old and we have to shift our allegiance to the laptop.

When we get home from our boat jumbling travels, we go to bed with a forecast of a strong blow during the night. This proves to be a gale with gusts in excess of 70 mph and when we get down to the boatyard in the morning the shed has jumped sideways about 8 feet. Although there are no ends in the building, it has acted as some sort of giant box-kite and a yacht that was sitting quite happily in its cradle alongside has been pushed into a very precarious position, with a significant lean. I am having kittens, and race to apologise to the yacht's owner. "Don't fret Lorraine," he says phlegmatically, "nobody died." What a star! Another new friendship is born. The yard staff spring into action and the forklift truck soon straightens everything out, with no damage done to anything or anyone. Phew! Within an hour the shed is secured in its original position with four industrial-size land anchors.

A land anchor

Our other boat neighbour, Fran, has a lovely classic wooden motor sailer. The three of us immediately know that we are going to be good friends and Fran is my essential female company in a very masculine environment. We share many coffee breaks talking about nothing and everything, crying on each other's shoulders as and when necessary.

Now firmly attached to the ground, we settle down to finish the shed build. Each end of the shed has its own complications. The back wall needs a large ventilating fly window built into it, and the front wall will consist mostly of a full-width 'door' which can be raised up and down to allow for ventilation and access. It has to be large enough to allow the yard travel hoist to drive in and get the finished boat out. We solve the problem of the full-width door by constructing a sort of giant horizontal blind. With a couple of ropes and pulleys we can haul up the entire door and secure it out of the way.

The shed is now watertight and we can sort out the lighting and power arrangements, with plenty of sockets and strip lights. We have salvaged old kitchen units and surfaces from friends and are able use them to fit a couple of workbenches, with a plethora of cupboards and racks for tools and wood. Last of all – my favourite bit – a length of surface where the kettle, coffee and tea will live. This is soon christened the 'staff canteen' and, as time goes on, the kettle is joined by

The fly window

a slow cooker as we start to eat all three of our daily meals on site. Within a couple of days everything is done, and our new home is ready for action. Give or take a few pounds, the shed build has cost about £1,000, but it's money well spent as it will allow us to build with confidence in most weather conditions. Hopefully we'll be able to recoup some of it by selling the shed on when Thea is complete.

The finished shed

One day, as we sit drinking coffee in our new 'canteen' we have a surprise visit from the local and regional representatives from Beta Marine, Nick Oxley and Steve Booth. Quite early on in the planning stage we had decided on a Beta 35hp engine. There were several reasons for this decision:

- The Kubota engine upon which the marinisation is based is the same engine that we had in our previous boat and which gave us excellent service for over twenty years.

- This is a low-tech, almost agricultural, unit that is widely used in various plant applications. There are no electronics involved in its running, and the cam shaft is chain driven, which we feel is preferable to the modern toothed rubber belt assembly.

- We also know from past experience that the engine is smooth and quiet, or as quiet as a diesel engine can be.

- The 35hp decided upon gives us roughly 8hp per ton, which, for a displacement motor vessel, should prove adequate to get up to about 7–8 knots.

- The final advantage as far as we are concerned is the fuel economy. When cruising at 2,000 of the 2,800 available revs we will consume 3 litres per hour. As previously explained, our chosen fuel tank capacity will give us around a 450-mile cruising range.

• The basic engine is marinised by other companies abroad, but Beta Marine is a British concern based in Gloucestershire and prove to be extremely competitive on price. The marinising parts, being manufactured here in the UK, should be readily available if needed in the future.

We had contacted Beta for details and costings some weeks previously and are pleased and surprised to see Nick and Steve actually turn up in the shed, after all it's only one of hundreds of engines that they sell. Over the next couple of hours we agree a package for the purchase and delivery of our engine. They are very interested in the project, though we only have a line drawing pinned on our noticeboard to show them. We are encouraged by their enthusiasm, which continues throughout and beyond the build.

Now, let's build a boat…

Time to get on with it

Beams, frames, duck!

Quackers

APRIL 2015
LAUNCH DAY MINUS TWENTY MONTHS

We have spent about a month laminating the deck beams ready to slot into the deck structure, burning the midnight oil up in the conservatory after a long day working on the build shed. And, hurrah, the twenty-two beams are now finished and safely stored at home. They look beautiful, and big! Although we only need a few to be the full length of 11 feet, the rest will be cut to size for the wheelhouse roof, the side decks and the stern deck. The striped effect

Buddy checking the finished beams

of the mahogany laminate is just lovely. We made beams like this for *Selene* and we know that, once they have been shaped and varnished, they will be a dream.

We take a big delivery from Robbins Timber – the plywood for the hull skin, the heavy section pine planks for the building bed and the mahogany for the hull frames, stringers, deck shelf, backbone and stem. Every arrival of the delivery lorry from Robbins is now an exciting event and always lifts our spirits with promises of the goodies within. Hearing it rattle across the hardcore is music to our ears, though there is also the ringing of a cash register as money leaves our bank balance.

As we lay out the timbers for the building bed, we realise that:

(a) The shed is on a considerable slope – this in itself is unimportant but comes as a bit of a surprise.

(b) The hull is going to be pretty big!

Of course, we know that the boat is going to be 30 feet by 11 feet, but the space taken up by the building bed within the shed gives us a sense of her cubic size. We choose particularly heavy sections of timber for the bed and we bolt these together, reinforcing all the joints with gussets of plywood. This is essential as the accuracy of the entire hull build will depend on the strength and stability of this structure.

It's only April but, when the

Robbins' first delivery

The building bed

sun is out, it is becoming obvious that the shed is going to get pretty warm – so much for heat reflective polythene. We beg and borrow old bed sheets from our long-suffering friends and drape them alluringly across the side wall that predominately faces the sun, creating shade to prevent warping of our valuable timber, not to mention giving some protection for us.

Around this point, Tom sustains what we believe at the time to be a very minor injury to one of his shins, whilst processing scrap timber for our wood burner at home. One of the pieces of timber he is cutting up with the chainsaw flies off and hits him on the leg. He thinks it's only a nasty bruise as the skin isn't broken, but he will be punished in the weeks to come for not paying more attention to it. Even now it is painful and, of course, is the only bit that he knocks on everything in sight.

With the building bed finished it's time to start work on the construction of *Thea*'s hull frames. We are very excited about this because finally we will actually be 'boat building' instead of 'shed building'. First of all, we fasten sheets of rough ply to the building bed and paint them with white emulsion. This creates a drawing board onto which we can transfer *Thea*'s frame plans to full scale. It's critical that all these measurements are deadly accurate, so they get checked and rechecked by me as we go along. We know it's really easy to make silly mistakes at this point that might later jeopardise the whole project. We have bought a new table saw from a local discount store specially to do the job of cutting accurate angles for the frame joints. This proves to be a false economy and we should know better. The job needs to be done to a high degree of accuracy and a cheap tool isn't up to the task. Tools like DIY planer/

A frame on the drawing board

thicknessers and power saws are just not good enough for heavier jobs. Eventually we decide to dismantle Tom's home workshop so that we can bring his ancient big DeWalt radial arm saw down and build it into a workbench in our shed. This saw cost us a small fortune about thirty years ago and has been a real workhorse ever since. It has been used extensively throughout our life together, and I wouldn't like to hazard a guess at how many tons of firewood it has also processed. Certainly, in this case, we got what we paid for in a good way. The effort to move the saw down to the shed will pay dividends throughout the build. That done, progress goes well and soon we have a stack of frames leaning against the shed wall. Again, the main impression is – don't they look big!?

Arrival of our well-used DeWalt radial saw

During all of our boat-building projects, Tom has always spent a few minutes each day checking out the boatyard skips. This has been productive on many occasions as one man's scrap is another's treasure. He likes to keep boxes of odd fittings, metal and other bits and pieces available as he often has to create one-off

Some frames

pieces of equipment. Skips are excellent sources of such bits and bats. We are delighted one day to find a half-scale decoy duck languishing in the pile. A bright yellow plastic duck, which we found in the River Dart, had graced *Selene*'s prow throughout her build and now 'Quackers' joins our little gang, sitting proudly on a shelf overlooking our progress.

While Tom is busy furtling in the rubbish, I am on the foreshore scavenging for seaweed. We have a large garden at home, which normally doesn't get much attention during the summer because we are usually doing boaty things. This year is going to be different as we are going to be based at home, so I

Quackers post

?|4 This place is a mess – put me back in the skip

Quackers keeping an eye

A successful boat jumble

am determined to try at least to improve the condition of our soil and grow a few vegetables. Seaweed will be most excellent to do this, so I gather big armfuls of it off the foreshore and dump it in front of the build shed. After hosing off the worst of the salt, I spread it out to dry, giving the boat shed a slightly *Pirates of the Caribbean* look. We collect the dried weed into boxes ready to take home and scatter lovingly over what will be our new vegetable plots.

Time for another fun day out – Beaulieu Boat Jumble. This was once the Mecca for boat jumbling aficionados – a massive showground of some three acres, full of goodies. We are really looking forward to our visit. Sadly, the once vast site is now a quarter of its original size with very little of interest, the Internet having stolen the market here as it has done on the high street. However we personally do quite well, and scurry home clutching all manner of shiny things – a stainless steel pulpit, a stainless double bow roller, six stainless stanchions, a bronze stopcock, plus an anchor light, a table leg, teak rings for the locker catches, a Jabsco accumulator tank for the freshwater system and a master battery switch. We probably didn't get as much as we'd hoped for, but it was worthwhile and a welcome change of scenery.

Fun time over, we start to fix the hull frames to the building bed. The plan is to build the hull itself upside down. A large amount of the hull skinning – the bottom for instance – is much easier to do looking down on it rather than up at it. As we assemble the frame structure there is lots of work for me to do double checking all measurements with a tape and a spirit level. Once all the hull frames are securely attached to the building bed, we use a 16-foot length of thin pine as a fairing batten to check the accuracy of the hull curves. Then all the hull frames are securely attached to each other on a temporary basis with lengths of 2 x 1-inch roof battening and screws. There are big sighs of relief when we find that everything lines up beautifully with very little needing to be done to fair things up. After cutting out the rebates to make the channel along which to laminate the backbone, we check the glued joints at the keel and, to our delight, they are completely free of voids – another sigh of relief. We retain the offcuts from the rebates to show the surveyor when he next visits.

Standing back to look at our work, I have to say we are just a little bit pleased.

The frames are set up

Thea's skeleton takes shape

Forefoot former

MAY 2015
LAUNCH DAY MINUS NINETEEN MONTHS

Busy, busy, busy. We are now doing the work that will complete the skeleton of the hull and we will be able to see *Thea*'s shape in three dimensions. The first job will be to laminate the backbone along the 'top' of the frames. This is going to be fashioned from three layers of 6 x 1-inch mahogany plank epoxied together to form a 6 x 3-inch solid piece, laid along the rebates that Tom has already cut in the frames. We are relieved to find that this is a relatively easy and satisfying piece of work that prepares us for some of the trickier shaping to come. Once the epoxy has cured Tom cuts the limber holes. These are the holes that are traditionally cut into the frames of a wooden hull, near to the keel, to provide drainage. Hopefully we'll never need them, but it's best to be on the safe side! It is much easier to cut them out at this point than it would be later.

To finish the central spine of the boat, we now need to fabricate a stem and forefoot, and connect them to the backbone. A lot of careful measuring shows us where the stem should be. The stem is one solid straight piece of mahogany and Tom supports it in place at the correct angle with some temporary battening. Then he has to make a 'former' – similar to our deck beam 'former' but much smaller. We bend thin sheets of mahogany over this to make the shaped piece

Backbone laminate showing limber holes

of timber that will be the fore-foot connecting the stem to the backbone. Using this laminated curve to bridge that gap proves to be a particularly hairy operation. Whilst fitting the 'curve', it is difficult to hold it in place and it attempts to do damage to itself and to us. We persevere using even more G-cramps to hold it in position, supporting its weight with a rope slung to the rafters of the shed. Finally, it's where it should be. It's still intact and some plasters sort out any damage to us. We have our bow – a really sweet entry line that we are delighted with. It looks and is solid and purposeful.

Completed forefoot laminate

Having temporarily finished with the bow, we move on to the transom. We are determined to incorporate curves into *Thea*'s hull wherever possible and this is

Stem and forefoot assembly

particularly important for the big area that is the transom. Leaving it flat is not an option as it would be visually rather crude. A series of curves will 'confuse' the eye and combine to soften the shape. The first of our pile of laminated beams is put in place as a transom deck beam. It is attached to the aftermost frame and will eventually create a lovely deck curve across the top of the stern. We now need to add a curve across the vertical face of the transom and Tom fits extra frames, which will allow us to add shape in that plane. The central one of these is attached to the backbone with a laminated timber knee, giving a very strong joint between backbone and transom.

Transom knee

I look at Tom as he is shaping the sides of the transom and am struck by the fact that he looks a bit pale. He tells me he feels faint, and then really quite poorly indeed. His shin, injured a month or so ago, has developed what we later find to be a subdural haematoma and, basically, he is being poisoned. It is a Sunday afternoon (of course!), so our surgery is closed. I drive him over to the Minor Injuries Unit at Torbay Hospital. The infection is bad enough that he has to have intravenous doses of antibiotics, delivered at the hospital, every day for a week. Then he will have to visit our surgery every week for a while to have the wound checked. Naturally, there is a hiatus in our boat work while he has his hospital treatment. I think he would have chosen to work through the whole incident, but the cannula through which the antibiotics are pumped has to stay in the back of his right hand and that makes any boat work impossible, even for a stubborn Welsh boat builder.

As soon as the cannula is removed I have no chance of keeping Tom at home, so it's back to the boat shed for the battle of the chines, which is something we'll never forget. Tom has cut the recesses in the frames to take the chine stringer and we start the challenging job of bending a single 1-inch thick, 5-inch wide mahogany plank along the length of the chine from transom to stem. This twists the plank in two directions, which patently it isn't terribly happy about. We use many G-cramps and rig a Spanish windlass to pull the reluctant plank into place. I have visions of flying metal cramps taking out our teeth if they give up under the strain. A Spanish windlass is simply constructed with a loop of rope laced around a secure point and the piece of timber you are dealing with. A length of timber or bar is then inserted through the loop and then wound. The windlass can create enormous power and is a proven way of drawing things together that don't really want to do so. Under normal circumstances it will be the wood you are attempting to move that will give way if there is a problem. However, the length of rope we are using is a second-hand piece we have been given and we don't really know its age. It is terylene and quite a heavy section, but using it proves to be an almost fatal error (literally). There is UV damage to the rope that isn't visible. Having set the windlass up, I spin the winding lever and Tom guides the length of timber into place. At one point there is a distinct 'tick tick' sound and Tom is horrified to think that the plank is splitting but, in fact, it is the rope on the windlass starting to break up and unravel. As he is perched precariously on a stepladder, he shouts at me to relieve the tension on the rope immediately before it disintegrates, which would let the plank fly back and hit him in the chest. The pressure on the plank at the time might well have caused a terminal blow and this is an example of how a well-planned job can suddenly go badly wrong. You are never more than one step from disaster!

Using a new piece of rope, and with a huge sigh of relief, we get the end of the plank glued and screwed into the stem. It's now definitely time to have a sit down, drink a cup of coffee and calm our shattered nerves. Still somewhat shaken, we are consoled by the beautiful line of the chine. Once we have this first plank under control it doesn't seem quite so scary to put on the second plank giving us a finished section of 5 x 2 inches. Holding the lamination in place while the epoxy glue goes off needs every G-cramp we have, plus some. Tom makes some extra clamps using bits of 2 x 1-inch wooden batten, threaded rod and some wing nuts. They work really well, and we use them many times during the build. Repeating the exercise on the other side is still taxing for our nerves but we now have confidence in our new piece of rope. We are living on adrenaline by now and can cope.

Flushed with success we turn our attention to the fitting of the deck shelves. This is much the same bending process, but the curves involved are not as violent or complex so it doesn't take as long to get them in place. Once again, these are a laminate of two planks of timber.

The final parts of our framework are the stringers – two laid along the bottom and one along each side of the hull – and suddenly our skeleton is complete. Standing back, we can see Thea in three dimensions, and it is a wonderful moment. The lines on Tom's now slightly grubby plan have become a real boat shape and some of the curves that have been produced are awesome.

Chine laminates showing DIY cramps

Bow, chine and stringers

I've lived with Tom now for over thirty years, but I don't take his skill for granted. This is already a major achievement.

I run around the boat shed looking at *Thea* from all angles – outside, inside, up ladders – taking more of the thousand photos with which we intend to bore our friends forever.

Boat skeleton completed

CHAPTER FIVE

A different way to fit a stern tube

Cutlass bearing

In which…

- **The stern tube is fitted**
- **The keel is built**

JUNE 2015
LAUNCH DAY MINUS
EIGHTEEN MONTHS

Fitting the stern tube doesn't sound like it would be too difficult a job but, on a wooden boat, the reality is a very sweaty operation. Quite a large and very accurate hole has to be bored through a lot of solid timber to take the bronze stern tube which will house the propeller shaft. In our case this hole is going to end up about 4.5 feet long and we certainly don't have any bits of engineering kit that will accurately bore a hole like that. In the past wooden boat builders would have had a specialist piece of equipment to do the job and might, if you were very nice to them, lend it to you. Nowadays, with the advent of GRP, it is nigh on impossible to find a boat builder with this tool and certainly there isn't one near to us.

Bucking convention we decide to fit the stern tube before we laminate up the keel. This will mean drilling only two relatively short holes – one through the sternpost and one through the backbone. These will take either end of the tube. Then we can fill in the hole around the stern tube once it is in place and the keel has been fitted. But these two holes will need to be accurate in themselves and in relation to each other. We'll have to have the angles correct to allow the stern tube to pass through and end up at exactly the right place for the shaft to be connected up to the engine. Once again, we'll have to take very careful measurements before doing anything irreversible.

Tom puts his thinking cap on and looks around for something that can be machined to make an exceedingly long hole saw of exactly the diameter of the proposed stern tube. In the end we buy a piece of basic heavy walled steel tubing of the appropriate measurements and Tom cuts a set of coarse teeth in one end. This is where he makes a classic error and carefully cuts the teeth angles in the wrong direction for the rotation of the drill. This means, of course, that they won't cut at all, and the whole operation has to be repeated with the teeth angled in the right direction. A stupid mistake, but these things happen – one of those occasions when you say: we'll laugh about this in years to come! The angle at which the stern tube needs to be set is lifted from the boat plans and now we must temporarily fit the sternpost. This is a heavy piece of iroko of appropriate measurements. After pre-boring it, we put it in place with temporary wedges, which will allow for fine line-up adjustment. The post fits in a hole that has been cut in the backbone, part of it ending up inside the hull. Then we set up a couple of plywood guides through which to run our new hole saw cutter at the correct angle. The driven end of the cutter is attached to a powerful electric drill by making a primitive universal joint with some bolts. Tom looks like some sort of crazed machine gunner perched up on the backbone, with the drill and its 'muz-

zle'. Thus, we can cut through the backbone with the guarantee that the hole will come through at exactly the right place in all planes. Although we know that our theory is sound, I have my heart in my mouth until the cutter finally breaks surface under the backbone and we can see that all is well.

Tom is pretty chuffed that his

DIY hole cutter

The stern tube hole boring assembly

answer to yet another problem is such a success. The admittedly rather Heath Robinson boring set-up proves that, with a little thought, complicated jobs can be done quite economically. The total cost for

a piece of bespoke boring equipment came to little more than £10.

It's time to run a piece of string through the holes for the proposed shaft/tube and check that the engine will be in the right place. Then we can fit a timber block under the backbone to give a face on which to mount the inboard shaft bearing. We are in a

Mounting for inner stern tube bearing

Extra laminates on stem

position now to fit the sternpost on a permanent basis and reinforce it with a floor running athwart ships inside to take its lateral stresses.

With that taxing problem out of the way we move on to fit the main length of keel. This is two pieces of 6 x 4-inch iroko, scarfed together to form one piece some 8 metres long and weighing about 38 kg. Consequently, it's an interesting exercise to get it in place, involving more ropes and tackles. There is an amount of shaving with a power plane to match the keel to the curve of the backbone before it is glued into place.

Now we can start to add extra laminates to marry the keel to the existing forefoot, and then additional timber to the stem onto which to fasten the plywood of the hull skin. Further sections of iroko are cut and shaped to fill the empty triangle between the backbone and the keel, leaving a gap for the stern tube. All of these sections are glued to the backbone assembly and to each other.

A welcome interruption is the exciting arrival of our shiny bronze stern tube, the inboard bearing and outboard cutlass-type bearing. We had to wait to order these until now, when we knew the exact

Gap in keel ready to receive stern tube

length of tube required. They are just lovely, all new and shiny, and I can't stop stroking them (sad, I know). I've always been a sucker for new pieces of beautifully engineered bronze work, and these are superb – art forms in their own right. The stern tube slides into place through our pre-drilled holes as though it has always been there, and the inboard and outboard bearings are fitted in place with bronze coach screws. That done we can fill in the gap between the backbone and the new keel. We do this from either side, hollowing out a half round groove that fits around the tube that is already in place. Once again, using epoxy resin has enabled us to fashion something as a solid section from several smaller pieces. This may not be a tradi-

Stern tube and inboard bearing

Finished keel with stern tube

tional solution, but it works well and avoids the very real, verging on impossible, problem of boring a long and accurate hole without the appropriate machining tools.

Time to drill through the keel, backbone and frames so that keel bolts can be fitted to tie everything together, which involves drilling every frame other than where the stern tube is – this has already been strengthened by the floor supporting the heavy sternpost, and by the sternpost itself.

And there she is – sporting her keel, stem and stern gear. One more step on the way.

Thea's shell is created

The 'hollow' forefoot

In which…

- **The hull skeleton is faired**
- **The plywood skin is applied to the hull**
- **The plywood is epoxy coated**

EARLY JULY 2015
LAUNCH DAY MINUS SEVENTEEN MONTHS

Yet another challenge. We are about to cover the skeleton of *Thea* with plywood – her 'skin'. But first we need to carefully 'fair' the whole framework, i.e. the frames, the backbone including the stem, the forefoot, the chines and the stringers. Fairing is important and involves shaping the faces of the framework to make sure that there will be maximum glued surface contact when the plywood sheets are curved around it. 'Good enough' is not good enough because any voids will compromise the strength of the hull.

The fairing baton comes into its own for this job and the use of a power plane speeds up what is inevitably a long and painstaking operation.

Now for the plywood. The ply we have chosen is marine quality supplied by Robbins Timber to guaranteed BS1088 standard. When we were choosing our timber supplier it became obvious that it is important to buy plywood from a trusted source because there is a lot of ply designated as BS1088 that is, in fact, no better than shuttering ply, being full of voids and held together with very suspect glue.

We decide to start attaching the plywood on the bottom of the hull – currently the top of the boat – working our way back from the bow. To give us a datum point, and an easy start, we lay our first sheet of ply just behind the severe and compound curve that leads to the forefoot. This point of the bottom is a reasonably flat area and presents few difficulties; the plywood is shaped to fit and simply glued and screwed to the frames, the backbone and the stringers. The 4-foot width of the plywood sheet doesn't quite reach the chine, leaving a gap that will be filled in with narrower plywood pieces later. This single sheet of ply is duplicated on the other side and now we are presented with what will probably be the biggest challenge of our construction so far.

The boat design calls for a hollow forefoot but this will be impossible to achieve with the plywood in sheet form. It would have to be bent into part of a sphere and patently a complete sheet of ply won't do that as it can't be bent in two directions at the same time. The solution is to revert to double diagonal construction, which is broadly the method we used to build the hull of our previous boat *Selene*. This time we'll be using 6-inch strips of plywood and epoxy instead of strips of solid timber and epoxy.

First sheet of ply goes on

Conveniently we can use two layers of 6 mm ply, laminated together, which will match the single thickness of 12 mm ply used for the rest of the hull. Bending the strips of 6-inch-wide, 6 mm plywood into the hollow shape of the bow form is quite easy and needs no forcing. The first layer of strips is simply nailed with brass pins onto the existing

Second layer of double diagonal on the bow

framework, bedded into epoxy. These strips cannot just be laid parallel to each other, because of the 'cone' shape. Each one must be scribed and cut to match its neighbour. For the second layer of ply, the strips must be laid at approximately 90o to the underlying skin. This time the plywood is bedded into epoxy and then screwed through both layers of plywood and the framework. The result is amazing, creating a bow section that normally is only seen on glass fibre boats. I know we are biased, but it really is pretty awesome – in fact, to us at least, breathtaking. We are very pleased with the result, and the fact that it is a difficult job behind us. The worry of getting this bit right has always been at the back of our minds.

Double diagonal construction was used for the building of lifeboats and for many of the utility powerboats in World War Two as it is a fairly easy and straightforward way of creating some quite complicated shapes. Back then they riveted the sections together, using paint-soaked canvas as a water-proofing agent between the layers. Our bow, therefore, is reminiscent of high-speed craft like air-sea rescue launches or motor torpedo boats. I show photos to my brother (Navy) who says, "Good grief, sis, you've built an MTB". Though *Thea* is not intended to be fast, this style of forefoot should cut cleanly through the water and create little resistance – more economical for us.

Whilst all this is going on up above, I am underneath tidying up all the drips and runs of epoxy resin that are seeping from miscellaneous joins and joints before the epoxy cures and becomes an absolute devil to clean up. To avoid the most permanent of perms, I am wearing a shower cap, or sometimes a plastic bag – I knew this would happen!

As we move into June the weather, and therefore the shed, is getting pretty hot. The specially bought heat reflective polythene used on the shed roof is working to a point but even so the temperature at midday is well over 30°C on the top of the hull. This makes our working conditions pretty difficult. The epoxy is curing too quickly and we are bordering on suffering heatstroke. In an attempt to provide shade, we scrounge more bed sheets and pin them to the roof framework. It's still not enough, and a friend lends us an industrial size fan to mount in the fly window at the back of the shed. We debate whether to use a slow-cure epoxy, but the temperature range between day and night is significant and we could compromise our progress if gluing jobs fail to cure overnight.

Even with the fan working hard and our attempts at shade, we cannot reduce the temperature enough to make working aloft tolerable.

We decide to call a halt on skinning the bottom of the hull (currently, of course, the top) and to work on the transom instead until the high-pressure system passes through and things cool down. The transom proves to be an easy job – bending sheets of ply around a single gentle curve – and it is much cooler closer to the ground working by the open shed front.

The lovely weather has worked it's wonders in our garden at home. Worms have reduced the seaweed I collected into a rich tilth, and we finally pick our very first strawberry. It's a whimsical little number, bearing a striking resemblance to a Scottie dog. We bring it down to the yard so we can eat it in the sunshine, sharing it on a single scone.

As always with the cycle of English weather, the high pressure passes and we are into cooler conditions. We can continue fitting the sheets of ply to what will be the bottom of the hull. This is where the use of large sheets of plywood demonstrates the speed of this type of construction, with the bottom of the hull being completed in two days.

Plywood on the transom

Starting to lay the plywood on the side of the hull

Moving on to the sides of the hull, the fitting of the ply is another fairly simple operation compared to the compound curves around the forefoot. We cut the plywood sheets to fit, then glue and screw them to the frames, the chine, the stringers and the deck shelf. For simplicity we join the sheets using a butt joint, with a backing pad of 12 mm ply behind it. The disadvantage of this could be that you have a none-too attractive piece of ply on the inside but, in our case, this will be hidden behind furniture or under the cabin sole. The glued reinforcing pad will be 6 inches wide and we are happy that this will give us a strong joint.

To add even more strength to the forefoot, with its double diagonal construction, we lay on two layers of woven glass cloth bedded into epoxy. This is the most likely part of the hull to suffer unintentional damage in the future and reinforcing it seems to be a good insurance policy. The rest of the hull will simply be painted with multiple layers of epoxy resin and not entirely coated with fibreglass cloth. All butt joints, though, are covered on the outside with a strip of woven rovings to provide extra strength. This system worked well for our previous boat, the timbers of which were still bone dry after twenty plus years, despite most of them being spent in the water. Skinning a hull completely with glass fibre and epoxy needs a fairly ambient temperature and humidity, and we have a far from perfect building environment that is not climate controlled. We'd rather avoid it if possible.

Carving bilge keels

Tom carves two solid pieces of iroko to form a pair of shallow bilge keels, which we add to the bottom of the hull. We are trying to retain a clean and unbroken underwater profile so that *Thea* will be easily driven, hence these keels are comparatively small. But they will be large enough to allow her to dry out safely if necessary, albeit at an angle.

The chines, and the join between the bottom, sides and transom, are now heavily radiused. The bigger the radius, the better the water will flow around the hull.

Bilge keels

Next, we sheath the hull, including the reinforcing strips, with five coats of epoxy. In order to maintain a wet edge while we are applying the resin, we work late into the cool of the evening. Overnight the temperature drops even further, as we are in an unheated polythene shed. Consequently, in between coats, the previous cured coat has to be washed with soapy water to remove the amine blush, which is wax that is included in some epoxy resins to aid curing. This occurs particularly if the resin cools below 10°C, which inevitably, in our circumstances, it does. This 'waxy' residue cannot be sanded away or over coated – it must be removed by soap and water, which is actually quite easy. The cured epoxy on the 'top' of the hull is like a skating rink between coats. We slither about trying to get purchase on the glass-like finish to avoid taking a tumble, not helped of course by the addition of soapy water! The building up of these coats of epoxy helps to fill in any irregularities on the hull, for example where the strips of glass fibre have been applied to the hull joints.

We fill and finish the bottom and the sides of the hull as this is so much easier to do whilst it is inverted. We have bitter memories of working a sander above our heads for hour after hour in the past and are definitely going to avoid it this time. There is some energetic fairing to get as smooth a finish as we can. Tom buys me my own personal sander to spread the joy. The end product is fine for the underwater sections, which will be coated with anti-fouling, but the top sides will need a lot more work in the future to produce the necessary near-to-mirror finish.

Finally, before turning the hull over, the keel and the forefoot are fitted with a stainless steel keel band, held on with a combination of Sikaflex and some really heavy gauge screws. The band will protect the keel from impact and any damage that might potentially be caused by drying out, as it will protect the waterproof epoxy coating.

And there she is – our finished hull, albeit upside down!

Stainless steel keel strip

CHAPTER SEVEN

A crane, skill and cunning

The right way up

LATE JULY 2015
LAUNCH DAY MINUS SIXTEEN AND A HALF MONTHS

The time has come to turn the boat over – a simple sentence to say, but one that needs some planning and some courage. First of all, we need to support the hull shell using temporary timbers to form a reinforcing structure inside that will take the wringing stresses of the turnover. We estimate that the hull shell and its reinforcing weigh around a ton, and it has to be able to survive the journey to the crane in the travel hoist, the turnover and the journey back to the build shed – all without any distortion of or damage to the hull. Once the supporting framework is in, we have to disengage the hull from the heavy building bed to which it has been securely attached, so that we can lift it free.

And then the day arrives – turnover day. This is an extremely stressful but very happy few hours.

The temporary internal bracing

The combined efforts of ourselves, the marina staff, the crane, a forklift truck, a travel hoist and several strong and enthusiastic friends will manage to extract *Thea* from her build shed, trundle her down to the dockside crane, turn her over and trolley her back.

Part of the design of the build shed is the capacity to remove a section of the front 'door' to allow the travel hoist to be backed into the shed, but we also have to remove all of the equipment, benches, saws and lumber that have accumulated around us to give it clear access. Fortunately, the work benches make an excellent tea station outside to supply refreshments to the assembling crowd of yard staff and friends that want to witness the event.

The hoist is backed in with impressive accuracy and speed. It has 3 inches to spare either side – some people really know what they are doing with large pieces of machinery. Suddenly *Thea* is in the air and moving rapidly down the boatyard towards the crane closely followed at the trot by our gang of helpers, with me hopping along at the rear shouting "wait for me, wait for me". It is unlikely that most yard hands ever experience the complete turnover of a boat, but ours step up to the mark and do an excellent job.

Once the hull has been transferred from the hoist into the slings of the crane, the slow and cautious business of turning her over can begin. First of all, one side of the hull is blocked up and

The audience!

Under the crane

Up she goes

Halfway

Nearly there

the slings are shuffled around to lift that side a little further up. This is repeated until the hull is at right angles to the ground, and then it is just a question of reversing the process to lower her down to the ground again. Throughout this process *Thea*'s entire weight is being taken on one short length of one side. This is all highly exciting and becomes a bit of a boys' day out with everyone wanting to get involved. The temporary internal structure is certainly tested and is well up to the task, with no ominous groaning, creaking or cracking. There is no damage to anyone or anything, which is a huge relief.

At last she is the right way up and we can get a true picture of what we've built – and most certainly it is good.

The building bed is dismantled in the now empty shed, and the sections stored off to one side ready to be used at a later point in the build. *Thea* is posted back inside to sit on some temporary chocks.

We can now reassemble the front of the shed and move all of our gear back inside. Then the painstaking process of truing up the hull in all planes begins. The easiest way of getting the fore and aft trim correct is to set up a length of string alongside the hull, running fore and aft, in an absolutely horizontal plane, and matching the waterline points on the bow and the stern to it. Getting the hull upright side to side is easier – we just lay a timber straight edge across the hull and put a spirit level on it. When this is complete, we chock the boat up securely in position, nailing the chocks together under the bilge keels to make sure that nothing moves whilst we are thumping around inside. She will stay like this until she is complete and ready to come out of

On her way back

Back home

the shed one final time. Again, time spent at this point is essential to get all the internal arrangements accurately built. The cockpit sole, for instance, must be built with a slight incline to allow it to self-drain. We can only ensure that if we know that the boat is entirely true.

We've laboured long and hard to get this far – some four months including the building of the shed – and we are pleased with our result. But we know from previous experience that building the hull is about a quarter of the job. Standing inside the bare shell reminds us that we have only just begun!

CHAPTER EIGHT

Thea takes shape and I fall apart

The first foredeck beam

EARLY AUGUST 2015
LAUNCH DAY MINUS SIXTEEN MONTHS

Now *Thea* is upright and secured in position, we take out some of the temporary structure inside her. The diagonal cross braces come out leaving only the horizontal cross members holding the boat in shape. This gives us the necessary space to work, whilst retaining the structural stability of the hull.

We set about fitting the raised deck shelf, which will support the foredeck. This goes in quite easily as it follows a relatively gentle curve, using the little homemade wooden clamps we made to set up the chine and main hull deck shelf. Gosh, but they have come in useful! This is another laminating job, producing the finished dimensions of the deck shelf, which are 4 x 2 inches, composing of two pieces of 4 x 1 inches. Again, it is essential that the two planks are held tightly together along the entire length while the epoxy cures, so having a large number of clamps is essential.

That done, we transfer all of our carefully made deck beams from the conservatory at home to the build shed and load them into the hull. We have had a couple of occasions when the high spring tide has made a little ingress into the shed, and we don't want to leave our precious hardwood beams on the ground where they might get a bit damp. One by one we fit them, starting at the point where the main bulkhead will be fitted, and work forward to the stem, leaving the necessary gaps where a hatch and the companionway will be. Whilst doing this, Tom is using a sheet of ply

The first beams go in - the scene of the plywood incident

Raised foredeck with beams in place

as a 'workstation', balancing it on the cross members. Suddenly the ply slips and deposits itself and a pile of tools into the bottom of the boat with a crash. Tom, using his panther-like reactions (!) is left hanging from the deck beam he has just fitted. The crash and Tom's sailor language bring other boat owners running to check on his well-being, but fortunately all is fine. Tom's leg is still giving him some trouble and his balance probably isn't all it could be.

All of the temporary cross members in this area can now come out as the beams have taken over the job of holding the boat together.

Having completed the beam installation in the forepart of the hull, we can now turn our attention to fitting the curved sections of the port and starboard deck shelves. These will eventually support the side decks and are composed of four thicknesses of half-inch ply mating the raised foredeck deck shelf to the lower one. We also fit the deck beam, to which we will attach the aft cockpit bulkhead and the stern deck.

That done we can install the main bulkhead, which will stand between the wheelhouse and the

Beam assembly for stern deck

accommodation under the fore-deck. Once this has been fitted, we can build off it to assemble the wheelhouse/cockpit sides, and the side deck framing.

Moving back to the stern deck framing, we fit three pieces of recessed ply, one on either quarter and one in the middle, which will provide under-deck reinforcing for two stainless steel bollards and a self-tailing winch.

Side deck framing

Sections of plywood are now fit-ted to form the side decks and the stern deck.

Skinning the side deck

With great relief we take out the remaining temporary cross members. Working amongst them has been a bit of a pain – sometimes literally – and it's lovely to have a clear space to work in without having to duck and dive. Are we the only people who constantly walk into things we know are there? I'm reminded of old black and white silent movies where the cast bump into walls, doors and scenery as part of the fun. It hurts a bit more in real life.

The foredeck is left unfinished at this point as there are several large sections of ply to be transferred from the ground up to and into the forward accommodation area. These will become bulkheads and semi-bulkheads, and it will be much easier if we can just 'post' them through the gaps between the beams, rather than try to shuffle them round bulkheads as they get built. Another advantage of leaving the foredeck unfinished is that, when fitting fair-sized pieces of plywood, we will only have two edges to fit – i.e. the bottom and the side(s), leaving any spare sticking up above deck level to be trimmed off later.

My hip is now becoming a serious issue. Climbing in and out of the boat is a bit of a challenge and I am pretty restricted to what I can do at ground level. I make a start with my power sander and do some rough fairing on the hull. To be honest, I don't get very far. An injection I have to try to minimise the pain in my hip only makes things worse and I'm in a bit of a state. I haven't slept properly for what seems like weeks and I just don't know what to do with myself. When we built *Selene* I had to work to earn the money to complete the build, and wasn't as involved as I would like to have been. Our plan has always been that we would build Thea together and I am distressed that I may be forced to take time out to have my hip replaced. I'm not worried about undergoing surgery, in fact I welcome it, but I want to stamp my feet in frustration. I don't, of course, because that would hurt too much!

Things to walk on

Fore hatch and foredeck

In which…

- **The forward bulkheads and semi-bulkheads are fitted**
- **The foredeck goes on**
- **The wheelhouse sole and accommodation are roughed out**

LATE AUGUST-EARLY SEPTEMBER 2015
LAUNCH DAY MINUS FIFTEEN AND A HALF MONTHS

As previously described, before we start work on the fore-deck, we fit the large bulkhead between the sleeping cabin and the galley. This operation is definitely made easier by posting the plywood through the 'roof'. The heads compartment is roughed out and the necessary semi-bulkheads fitted. At the same time, we fashion a box section support under the point where the mast step will be. This will take the compression of the mast. The box section later becomes part of the galley lockers.

Part of our design is to have a stubby mast of some 15 feet, mounted on the foredeck. This will carry:

- Our steaming light
- A spreader light to illuminate the foredeck
- The VHF/GPS aerial
- An anemometer (we use this on a regular basis to determine wind strength and direction when anchoring)
- A radar reflector

Heads semi-bulkheads

It will be useful to have all of these instruments and lights higher than deck level to give greater VHF range, better visibility for the steaming light and, when appropriate, the anchor ball.

All our semi-bulkheads and fitted furniture will be fitted to 'bulkhead standard', becoming part of an increasingly strong egg box construction within the hull.

Now that all the largest bulkheads are in, we can fit the plywood on the foredeck. Once again, we are

Deck beams and forward bulkheads

Mast compression post

cutting and fitting large sections of plywood, gluing and screwing them to the beams and to the deck shelves. This is another one of those jobs that has a huge result for not too much effort.

To finish off the hull skin, we now need to fill in the space between the existing hull and the raised foredeck with plywood, cutting the ply oversize to extend 2 inches above the deck to form raised toe rails. Suddenly, *Thea* has a rudimentary 'inside'.

The damage that was done to Tom's leg earlier in the year has still not healed and we are starting to become a little concerned. There is an open wound on his shin, which occasionally blows bubbles! We show it to a pharmacist who is frankly appalled and asks us to take it away. So we get Tom referred to a 'Lower Limb Therapy' unit in our local cottage hospital. This unit is run by a group of amazing therapists; ladies full of fun and jollity. We are constantly reminded of the Fascinating Aïda trio whose performances always reduce us to tears of laughter. These nurses are experts in their field and their opinion is that the infection, untreated, could start to compromise the bone in the shin. Tom doesn't want to end up like Long John Silver so he agrees to at least six weeks of compression bandaging. This is very hot and uncomfortable for him, but it finally does the job, though the whole experience leaves him with a large and manly scar. Being a rough, tough boat builder, though, he con-

Foredeck skinning

tinues to work through the treatment, protecting his leg with a footballer's shin pad. This episode has been a salutary lesson in taking care of yourself and being careful with any injury.

We treat ourselves to a half-day break to watch the Historic Flight perform as part of the air display at Dartmouth Regatta. There is a really good view from the picnic area at the boatyard and we set up our hampers with a bunch of friends and enjoy the display. We love the Historic Flight, and there is no better setting than the River Dart in which to watch the low and slow approach of the Spitfire, the Hurricane and the Lancaster, with the menacing roar of their engines.

The next major construction project is the wheelhouse, and we are very excited when the hardwood timber arrives. Sadly, and unusually for our suppliers, it is warped and has to be returned. Robbins are very good and promise that replacement supplies will be with us shortly, which, indeed, they are.

Another boost to our morale is provided by a visit from our surveyor. We have commissioned an in-build survey report to ensure that *Thea* is able to satisfy insurance underwriters and to maximise her valuation. The surveyor confirms that he is more than satisfied with the work to date. Yippee!

In the meantime, Tom, who is now working for two of us, starts to rough out the wheelhouse. The engine is going to be fitted underneath the cabin sole in the wheelhouse, so the first job is to fit the timber bearers for the engine bed using, once again, our piece of string as a lining-up guide. Two heavy sections of Columbian pine are shaped and bolted to the hull frames. All the earlier efforts to accurately line up the stern tube now prove their worth as the engine will fit very neatly into the predicted space, the sump just clearing the frames – as calculated.

The aft wheelhouse bulkhead is fitted at this point, together with the cabin sole framing. One

Engine bed

Wheelhouse after bulkhead

of the heavy baulks of timber that we saved from the building bed is cut down to form the beams that are going to support the wheelhouse floor. The level of this floor has been cunningly calculated to be higher than the engine, but as low as possible to maximise headroom between it and the designated height of the wheelhouse. The line drawing we are working to gives us a fair idea of what goes where but, once again, Tom always measures and remeasures to make sure things will fit. He cuts and installs the plywood sheets that will form the floor but leaves them unsecured to give us access for fitting tanks and ballast pods at a later stage. This also creates a very handy building platform for working on the wheelhouse structure.

Framing for port side wheelhouse cabin sole

Framing for starboard side wheelhouse cabin sole

Three coats of epoxy go onto every interior surface of the hull in the wheelhouse, whilst we have full and easy access to it. This complements the exterior coats of epoxy by protecting against any water ingress from inside the boat.

Although I've written this chapter as though I'm there, which I am of course in spirit, I'm spending most of my time at home unable to move about very much and trying not to feel glum. My days are enriched by visits from friends who manhandle me out of the house in a wheelchair and into their cars to do something I've never done in my life. I briefly become a 'lady who lunches', or visits coffee shops. Actually, I am amazed by the number of people of all ages that we meet who have either had hip replacements or are waiting to have one. One of our favourite haunts becomes a weekly meeting place for the exchange of 'joint' stories – all of which are highly entertaining and give me a deal of comfort.

Fortunately, I can still access the Internet and I'm able to save considerable amounts of money by working through our list of 'must haves' and finding the best suppliers. Costly domestics like the fridge, the cooker and the toilet arrive in quick success, the fridge coming from Germany. They can supply this fridge and deliver it far more reasonably than we can source it at home. This is all very exciting, and our new goodies start to pile up on the table in our sitting room just begging to be admired.

Wow – a wheelhouse!

Window framing – port side

LATE SEPTEMBER–OCTOBER 2015
LAUNCH DAY MINUS FOURTEEN AND A HALF MONTHS

Tom is starting on the satisfying job of finishing the construction of *Thea*'s wheelhouse. We are using solid iroko for the window frames and the door frame as varnished iroko gives a fair imitation of teak, without the expense. When the construction is finished all the hardwood of the wheelhouse will be coated with layers of epoxy on the outside, and then varnished. The epoxy we are using is not UV resistant, and needs to be overcoated with paint or varnish to protect it.

The port and starboard wheelhouse sides are machined and assembled off the boat, and then fitted on top of the existing plywood sides. Once these are finished, the window frames and the door frame

Framework for the wheelhouse windows

for the back of the wheelhouse are fitted.

The next move is to fit the remaining laminated beams to form the framework for the wheelhouse roof. The last, but not the easiest, task is to work out the geometry for the three front screens, the middle one of which will be an opening fly window and then, of course, to build and fit them.

The wheelhouse door is also machined and assembled, but not fitted at this point as we still need good access into the wheelhouse for engine installation and for moving other gear around.

Now we can skin the wheelhouse roof with plywood. This is another job where a small amount of effort brings visually spectacular results. It is a big roof, and will eventually house the handrails, navigation lights and a large solar panel. We extend the roof over the front screens, rather like a baseball cap peak. This will provide shade for the instruments around the helm and avoid them getting cooked by direct sunlight. Similarly, the roof extends some 2 feet over the cockpit to provide shade and shelter. Though, of course, the wheelhouse is still in an unfinished state, we are getting a very good idea of how *Thea* will look, and we are thrilled.

Wheelhouse window and door frames

Fitting deck beams in wheelhouse roof

A large and teetering pile of plywood offcuts has now developed. This is obviously quite attractive to people looking for small bits of ply for their own projects, but

Wheelhouse fly window frame

most of this wood will be used during the fitting of furniture and other parts of the interior fit-out so, reluctantly, we have to tell them that it isn't available. As a matter of interest, we were left with very few timber scraps at the end of the project, considering the amount of plywood, hardwood and softwood we had to buy.

We have another visit from our surveyor, who gives us his latest 'OK' to our progress. He is an experienced and renowned marine surveyor from the Solent, and we are very pleased to get his approval. He spends more time than is really necessary talking to us about our work and progress, which brings a lovely sense of pride.

Meanwhile, I am still at home buying yet more shiny bits like some kind of demented magpie. As the bank account empties, our lounge at home and the boat shed fill with a chart plotter, the VHF/AIS receiver, the Fish Finder, the helm assembly, the fuel tank, the water tanks, the propeller, the engine shaft and the bronze rudder mount, to name but a few.

Tom starts to fill in the large unfinished hole that will be the cockpit. The framework for the bench seats and cockpit sole goes in, using more pieces salvaged from the building bed. Then he cuts and loose fits the cockpit sole itself. This will not be secured at this point as, once again, we need to retain ease of access to

Wheelhouse overhang - aft

the bilge. But having the sole there will make it easier to work.

The locker lids in the bench seats will give access to two large 7-foot-long cave lockers where the boat's equipment will be stored – warps, fenders, jerry cans for water and fuel, and all the other paraphernalia that ends up being necessary.

The lockers under the stern deck where the gas bottles will be stored are now built. These will have the same self-draining capability as the cockpit and as such are ideal places to put the gas bottles and the petrol for the outboard. Any leaks from either will naturally vent overboard – a good safety feature.

Tom fits a hatch in the cockpit sole, which is designed to give easy access under the cockpit. This will enable us to check and service steering gear and the exhaust system in the future, as necessary. It will also be a good place to store the cockpit cushions.

We now have a structurally complete boat shell. So, with a big sigh of relief, we draw a line under that phase of construction – now to finish it off!

Wheelhouse roof overhang - forward

Thea's heart and lifeblood

Engine bed

In which…
- **The engine arrives**
- **The fuel tank is fitted**

NOVEMBER-DECEMBER 2015
LAUNCH DAY MINUS
THIRTEEN MONTHS

Thea's engine is due to arrive today, and Tom has managed to manoeuvre me down to the yard to witness the event. We have assembled a few friends to be available to help us move the engine about once it is on board and in the cockpit.

Once again, the yard's forklift magically appears and carefully extracts our engine from the back of the engineer's van. There are wildebeest-like grunts of approval from the chaps and squeaks of "ooh, it's very red" from the ladies.

A little bit of mucking about with a heavy piece of timber and some rope extends the reach of the forks on the forklift so that the engine can be lifted. Then it, and its crate, are manoeuvred over the

Engine being craned over the stern

stern deck and into the cockpit. Once this has been done, we use a length of scaffolding pipe and our strong friends to carefully muscle the engine through the wheelhouse door and deposit it safely on the cabin sole over the engine bay area. Offering heartfelt thanks, we wave goodbye to our chums, hoping they are not stumbling away in search of a truss. Tom attaches a chain hoist

Engine in the cockpit

to a temporary gantry and connects it to the engine. It is now a one-person job to raise and lower the motor as necessary for the final fitting in the engine bay. This involves fine juggling with some spacer pieces under the flexible engine feet to ensure that the gearbox and prop shaft line up correctly. Once in place the engine is left on its bearers and covered with a dustsheet. It can now be more or less forgotten about whilst the next phase of construction is started.

The whole of the space under the cockpit sole is painted ready to begin work on fitting the fuel tank and the exhaust system. As mentioned before, this is so much easier to do when the cockpit sole is still removable.

The mounting framework for the fuel tank is designed, assembled and painted, and then some pieces of carpet are fitted. These will protect the tank from possi-

Engine hanging from the chain hoist over engine bay

ble chafe. We have always had stainless tanks in the past and we have no experience with ones made of polythene. We want to give it all the protection we can. That done, the 215-litre (40-gallon) polythene

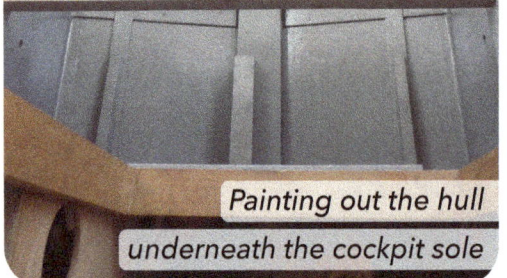

Painting out the hull underneath the cockpit sole

tank is dropped into place and secured. We have chosen polythene and not stainless steel this time because there will be less of a condensation problem inside. This should reduce the likelihood of diesel bug contamination in the future. These days, 'off the peg' polythene tanks are available in a range of sizes, avoiding the need for 'bespoke' and highly expensive stainless steel tanks.

We have included in the exhaust system a water trap, silencer and swan-neck. With the cockpit sole removed, all these elements of the exhaust system are plumbed in and secured while we still have plenty of room in which to fight with a thick and uncooperative rubber pipe. These three pieces of kit should take the 'bark' out of the exhaust – we know from previous installations that they produce a very quiet system.

The cockpit construction now proceeds apace. The plywood sole is glued and screwed down and a smaller locker constructed to give access to the top of the fuel tank where the fuel pipes and dipstick will be situated. This little locker will eventually house the fuel filler pipe, the filler cap and the stern gland greaser. It also proves to be a very convenient space in which to keep fuel funnels, fuel additives, and assorted dieselly rags so that they don't contaminate clean lockers.

Fuel tank in place

It's coming up to our first and indeed only Christmas in the build shed. We have a mahogany panelled lounge and a log burning stove at home – a room made for Christmas — and normally we would have a real Christmas tree. I can't face that this year and friend Paul takes me over to a store to buy the biggest and best artificial tree we can afford. By chance, chums Ian and Lyn are 'between boats and houses' and come to stay with us for the holiday. This is such a relief to me as doing the full Christmas bit in my current condition would have been a bit of a challenge. But the four of us have a lovely silly time, with copious amounts of luscious food and far too much alcohol. Tom and I agree that the next twelve months will be amazing, with the operation to relieve my pain happening in a couple of weeks and the completion of *Thea* scheduled before the end of the coming year.

Fuel locker under construction

Fuel filler in cockpit fuel locker

It would be easy to give up

Radiused corner

LATE DECEMBER 2015– EARLY JANUARY 2016
LAUNCH DAY MINUS ELEVEN AND A HALF MONTHS

It's now pretty much mid-winter and the weather is cold and wet – not unexpected really but it's making working in the build shed a bit tough. The polythene roof drips with condensation for half the day, and we have persistent rivulets of water running across the shed floor as water drains down from the land and the railway embankment. Our cunningly fashioned drainage channels are overwhelmed.

Tom decides to try and make the wheelhouse weather-tight so that the accommodation can be heated. Then there will be at least one comfortable area to work in and progress can continue. To achieve this, he needs to fit the wheelhouse door and the glass in the windows. The window spaces are measured, and we put in the order for the glass. We are using laminated glass, which is not unlike that in modern car windscreens. In the event of a pane getting broken, which is bad enough, at least anybody on the other side of it will not be treated to a face full of flying shards. While he is waiting for it to arrive, Tom mounts the wheelhouse door ready to receive its pane of glass. Then he starts work on the framework that will support the glass, by fitting the fixed glazing bars to the wheelhouse framing. This involves, in part, the manufacture of over one hundred and thirty neat little radiused corner pieces and a couple of hundred feet of iroko beading. The method will be to glue and pin the outside glazing bars to the main iroko structure, and then set the glass and the inner glazing beads into Sikaflex on the inside, held in place by brass pins.

Wheelhouse door and port side windows

Over the Christmas break (Tom does take Christmas Day off) he shrouds the wheelhouse in a cov-

Forward wheelhouse screen

ering of protective plastic sheet and puts a heater inside. The temperature is raised enough to care-fully apply three coats of epoxy resin to seal the new beading before the glass is put in, rubbing down between coats. Applying the resin takes three days but when he removes the plastic sheet all the epoxy resin, which should be clear, has gone cloudy due to the high humidity in the air. There is much sailor language. The result is totally unacceptable as all this hardwood will have a clear varnish finish even-tually. It takes him two days to scrape and sand off the offending resin. So, basically, working through Christmas has been a complete waste of time. Temporarily we will abandon the glazing part of the project until the weather improves and start on the engine bay fit-out instead.

Tom begins the installation of the fixed sound insulation in the engine bay. We have decided to fit 2-inch insulation on every surface throughout the engine bay, except on the hull. Panels of this insula-tion material are available in 2-inch thickness but – from a costing point of view – the 1-inch variety is proportionally cheaper as is it more commonly available. So we use two thicknesses of 1-inch insulation, found at a boat jumble at a discount price. The actual fitting of the insulation involves creating shallow boxes by screwing sections of 2 x 1-inch wooden batten on edge to the existing bulkheads and semi-bulkheads. Once the insulation is fitted into these boxes, it will all be covered by sheets of 6 mm ply to encapsulate it. This gives a good surface in the engine bay to paint, and also something on which to attach lighter fixtures and fittings. These will hold, for instance, the lengths of cabling involved in the electrical system. Then the four big pop-out panels for engine access are constructed, filled with the same high-tech sound insulation sheets, and painted. These, once finished, are somewhat heavy and unwieldy but they will give easy accessibility to the whole of the engine bay area. Three of these panels form the cabin sole over the engine bay and the fourth fits into the front forming part of the forward bulkhead.

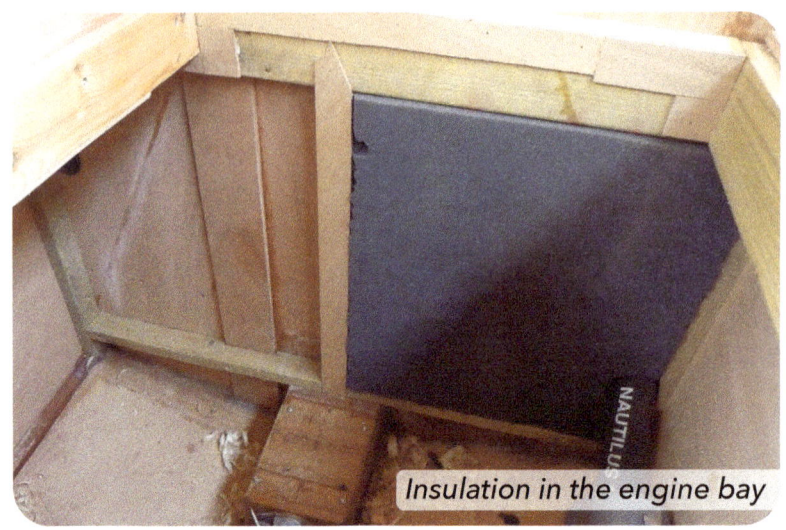

Insulation in the engine bay

Insulation on engine access panel

We expect all this insulation to reduce engine noise to a minimum, which is important as we will be standing on top of the engine bay in the wheelhouse when we are underway. Any engine noise will turn the wheelhouse into a sound-box – not a good idea. Nowadays, with efficient sound insulation, there is no need to tolerate a noisy boat engine. On any boat, the less intrusive the machinery noise, the more pleasant the travel will be.

Engine access panels

While Tom has been battling with the ups and downs of his lonely sojourn in the shed, he receives the first of a number of unexpected visits from a pair of local Jehovah's Witnesses. Now, this is something he wouldn't normally look for or welcome, but these people are a delight. As an ex-sailor the older chap, in particular, is fascinated by the work on the boat. Every visit follows the same routine – he hands over his obligatory leaf-let and then sets to questioning Tom in depth about his progress on the boat since his last visit. What a lovely man. He'll never know the encouragement we got from his approval.

Meanwhile, back at home, I go into hospital to have my full hip replacement operation. I am lucky enough to have a superb and very experienced orthopaedic sur-geon, and the whole procedure goes extremely well. I will follow my exercise routine and after-care instruc-tions to the letter and should be back in the boat shed within three months. My surgeon is very im-pressed by our project and calls me his star patient. I'm sure he says this to all the girls but it's good to hear and encouraging after what has been a very difficult and tiring few months. Although I can't pre-tend the experience didn't involve a degree of pain, the time in hospital – with doses of morphine – was the best rest I'd had for some considerable time. There were people fussing round, being wonderfully kind and feeding me lovely food with delightful regularity.

CHAPTER THIRTEEN

Getting back on our feet

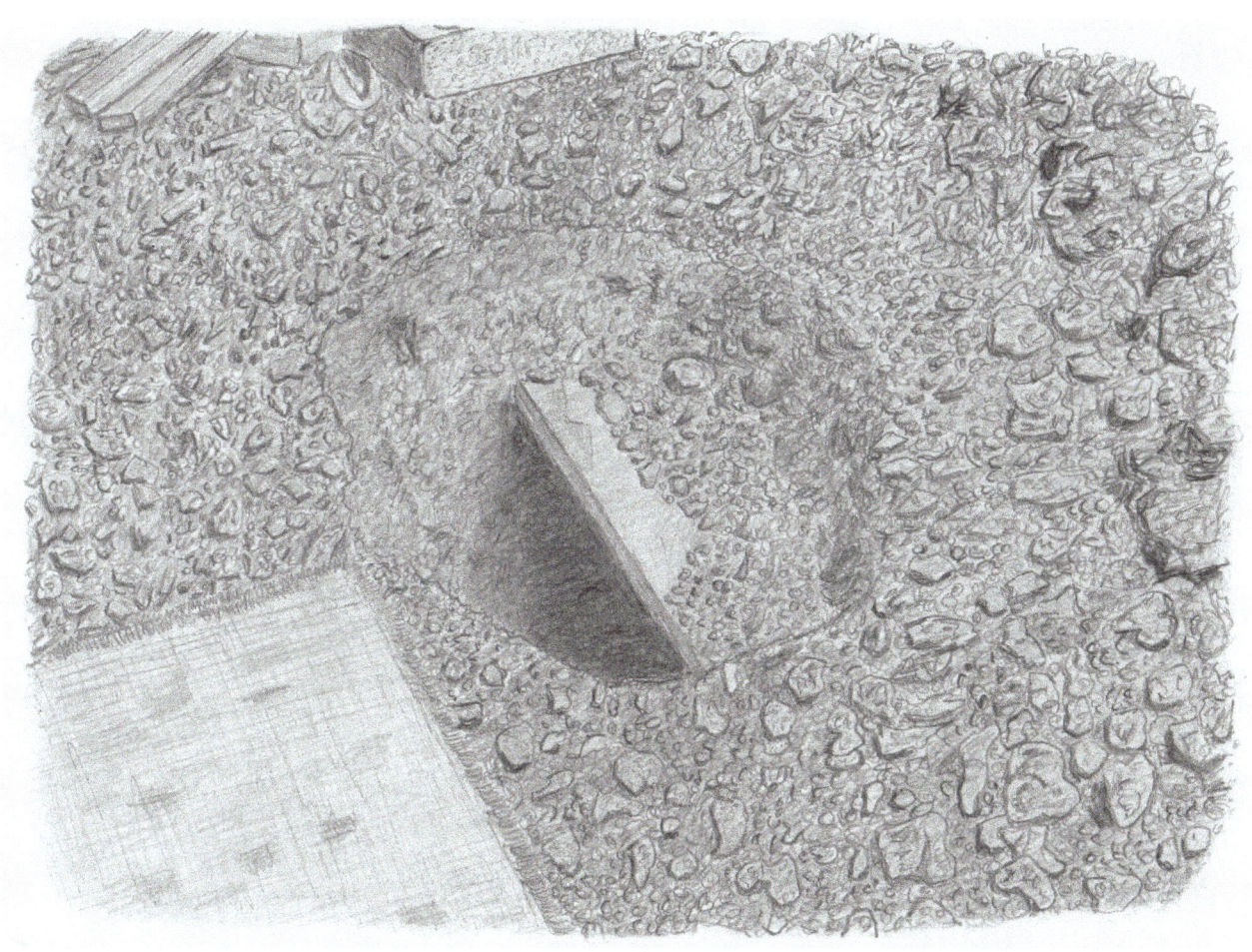

Digging hole to fit rudder

LATE JANUARY 2016
LAUNCH DAY MINUS TEN AND A HALF MONTHS

Sorting out *Thea*'s newly insulated engine bay is our next priority. Tom makes and fits mounting brackets for various pieces of equipment. These include the mountings for the Webasto heater, filters and fuel lines, and a sturdy box to house two large lead acid batteries. One of these will do duty as the domestic battery, and the other is a dedicated starter battery for the engine. A multi-position battery switch will be fitted later to give us the option to use either one, or both batteries.

We have chosen a Webasto blown hot air heating system as it can be mounted in the engine bay and therefore will not take up valuable space in the lockers. The heater unit runs on diesel, which we will be carrying on board for the main engine, and only uses approximately two litres per twenty-four hours. There are two methods of installing these heaters. One draws the air from outside and heats it to blow into the accommodation. The second is a recycling system which just circulates the air that is inside the cabin. We prefer the former as the fresh air drawn into the boat will displace any damp that may be created in the living space, forcing it out through the deck ventilators. From the information we've read, if it is installed properly, the Webasto is pretty well fool-proof and maintenance-free – here's hoping! We plan to install the exhaust system for this unit against the after bulkhead and run it out of the wheelhouse roof, rather than having it exit through the side of the hull as suggested in the installation instructions. Discussions with the manufacturer confirm that this is a safe modification and it will avoid any possibility of shipping seawater down the exhaust pipe. This, of course, would do the heater no good at all.

A section of plywood, which will act as a removable floor, is fitted over the prop shaft and inner shaft bearing housing. This will give secure footing for servicing the fuel filters and the after sections of the engine. Tom always does his own engine maintenance and is very interested in ensuring that a somewhat tedious job is safe and not too uncomfortable.

The engine is now hoisted out of the engine bay and Tom has some enjoyable days preparing and cosmetically finishing the whole engine bay with a large red lump swinging gently above his head (and occasionally making contact with it!). The bilge sections of the engine bay can now be sealed with

Painted engine bay

three coats of epoxy resin making it oil and waterproof. Once sanded down lightly, the entire area receives the necessary coats of paint and is finished with two coats of magnolia gloss. All of our interior paintwork, other than the bilge paint, will be magnolia gloss. We used this in *Selene*, and were particularly pleased with the finish, being much gentler on the eye than white paint.

It takes some time to track down the right 'shade' of paint. The first magnolia we buy is much too yellow for our taste, and reminds me of the smoke-stained pub ceilings of my youth. Our local decorating supplier steps up to the mark. I take them a twenty-year-old paint can left over from *Selene*'s build, which now has nothing but flakes of dried paint in it. They mix a batch of something they call 'orchid', which matches the flakes exactly. It's the bees' knees – just what we wanted – but we'll still call it magnolia!

We paint the engine room with this light-coloured paint to make a brighter workspace for servicing. Also, any possible spillage or drips from the engine can be readily traced and cleaned up. Tom is fanatical about the cleanliness of his engine bay. Too many boats smell of diesel when you go on board and, in our experience, nothing makes people 'heave' more quickly that a whiff of diesel. This is invariably down to spilt fuel somewhere around the engine and a failure to clean it up. The engine is our only form of propulsion and we want to make sure that it continues to work.

Engine being lowered into engine bay

Battery box in engine bay

Engine in engine bay

Spotting any problems like drips or leaks before they become a disaster will be easier in a clean and light area. Once the painting out has been completed the engine, which has been hanging like the sword of Damocles over the engine bay, is lowered onto its beds, lined up with the prop shaft and bolted down. When I visit the boat and see our lovely red engine sitting in its bright light engine bay, I am really stunned by the aesthetic effect of the contrast between the red and the 'magnolia'. Mechanical things don't have to be good to look at, but this is really the business.

Tom has been in discussion with the engineers who are supplying our stern gear and rudder system. We already have the rudder tube, which needs to be fitted before the final design of the rudder and its stock is agreed upon. After some more careful measuring, a hole is bored through the backbone in which to fit the tube. With this in place, final and accurate measurements for the rudder and its stock can be taken. These are sent off to our engineers who then manufacture a solid stainless steel rudder and stock.

Now comes the interesting job of fitting the rudder into its tube. This must be done from the outside of the boat and it involves digging quite a large hole (about 3 feet deep) to drop the rudder assembly into before it can be fed up the tube into its correct position. A relatively easy bit of digging becomes much more complicated when Tom strikes a large piece of half-inch-thick steel sheet some 6 inches below the shed floor. Luckily, by a bit of extra excavation, we can work round the edge of the sheet. This allows the rudder stock to go up into its tube and into position. The part of ground on which the shed stands at Noss boatyard is land that was reclaimed from the river many years ago. They literally dumped all the boatbuilding refuse under some hardcore, in the days before such things were frowned upon. Like a homing pigeon, Tom has unerringly dug his hole right on top of a bit of something of unknown, but certainly dubious, origin. Lucky it wasn't one of the bombs dropped here during the war!

Inside the boat the rudder stock is fitted with a plummer block, which supports the top of the stock and secures the rudder in the correct place. The final piece of work is to attach the bronze tiller arm to the top of the stock ready for the steering cable to be attached. Also, and quite importantly, we fit two rudder stops so that the steering gear cannot be strained when the boat is going astern. These will be set up to give approximately 40 degrees of movement of the rudder blade either side of the centre line. The last job for the rudder is to add a stainless steel skeg, which is mounted between the back of the keel and the bottom of the rudder shaft. This is not intended to support the rudder but is there to ensure that any ropes or other flotsam cannot be

Hole being dug to enable fitting of rudder

Rudder stock, tiller arm and plummer block

easily dragged up into the propeller and/or snag on the rudder.

So, there we go – engine in and rudder fitted. Meanwhile, as Tom slaves away, I am recovering at speed. The dressing has been taken off my hip and I can finally have a shower. By walking and doing my exercises religiously, I've managed a one-mile walk with my crutches in the sunshine. I'm counting the days before I can get back to work. My search for boaty bits on the Internet continues…

Rudder assembly

CHAPTER FOURTEEN

Tanks, seats and the return of Hopalong

Navigation table

FEBRUARY 2016
LAUNCH DAY MINUS TEN MONTHS

The last spring tide, which has been particularly high, brings yet more water into the build shed. In fact, one evening Tom comes out of the boat and down the ladder and just avoids stepping into water some 6 inches deep. He has to take his shoes and socks off to get out to the car, which is sitting in even deeper water in front of the shed. I open the door to him when he comes home, and he is standing there with bare feet and bare legs up to his knees – looking somewhat blue. Luckily, no damage is done to the boat, to the shed, to the car or, indeed, to Tom. Winter is starting to bite now and some days it's just so cold in the shed that he has to finish early and come home to warm through. Trying to heat the shed – or even the boat – is a waste of time as the warmth dissipates as quickly as we can produce it. Gas or diesel space heaters could raise the temperature, but they would produce unwanted damp.

Still, on most days, work goes on. The next move is back in the wheelhouse and involves the preparation to install two water tanks, one on the starboard side and one on the port side, under the sole. Before these can go in some serious reinforcing has to be constructed. Each tank will weigh roughly a quarter of a ton when full. The under-floor spaces where these will be fitted will also eventually be the home for roughly half a ton of ballast in the form of concrete blocks. Again, some of the now redundant building bed is sawn up and a heavy wooden base resembling

Hull reinforcing for water tank and ballast

a pallet is built. The hull and all this timber receive two coats of grey bilge paint. Holes are cut in the main bulkhead where the water tank pipework will eventually run. The starboard tank is now slid into position and secured with sturdy pieces of timber and ply to ensure that it can't move around.

Now this is done the rest of *Thea*'s dinette berth, which is only partially finished, can be completed. The bottoms of the lockers that have already been built are removable so there is reasonable access to the water tank and to the ballast area. The dinette assembly is raised some 8 inches above the floor level of the rest of the wheelhouse so that, when we are sitting around the table, we will have a clear

and unrestricted view through the windows – one of our 'must have' design features. Part of the dinette structure is a ply-wood box ventilation duct leading from the engine room and up the after bulkhead to a ventilator opening into the cockpit area. This ventilator will allow the heat from the engine room to vent to the outside and stop any condensation problems on the machinery. It is also the place where the Webasto exhaust pipe (previously mentioned) is fitted on its way to exiting through the wheelhouse roof. A shallow locker is built under the table base where the cushion that makes the dinette into a double berth can be stored when not in use. With this, the roughing out of the dinette area is completed for the moment.

Storage lockers under dinette seats

Dinette area

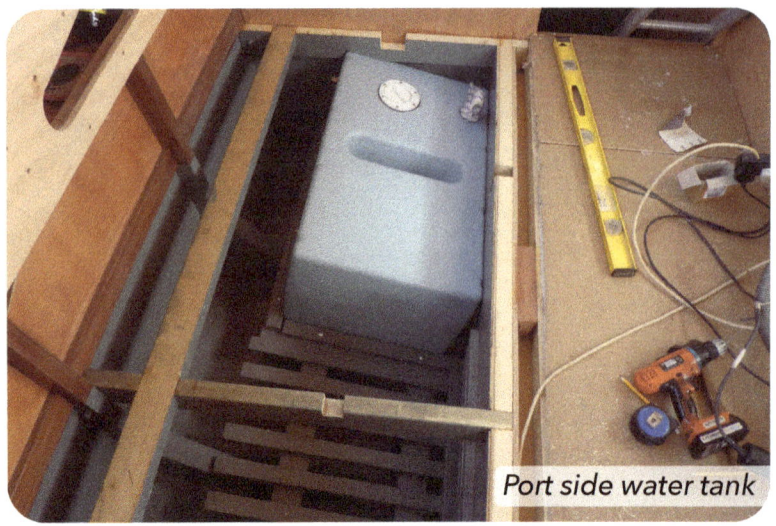

Port side water tank

It's time to move across the boat and fit-out the port side of the wheelhouse. First of all, the port water tank. Fitting this is more or less a repeat exercise of the starboard side. Skin fittings and inspection hatches have been fitted to both water tanks before they are installed. Once it is in place the port side cabin sole can be finally fixed down, though a section of the sole will be left as an access hatch to this under-floor section. Also, a small hatch is cut in the part of the sole that is directly above the inspection hatch of the water tank in the, hopefully, unlikely event that we need to clean out the tank.

That completed, Tom starts work on the furniture on the port side. This starts off with a box-like structure that has eight lockers for storage, and which will also serve as the base to mount the helm seat on. Aft of this Tom builds a small navigation area, with a hanging locker for coats, wellingtons and hats. Included in the assembly is a floor-to-ceiling vertical timber handrail which sits approximately midway through the wheelhouse. We consider handrails and grab bars to be vital on boats, giving you something to hang onto when the going gets rough. I was once on a friend's boat when it was heeled over. There were no handholds and I was stuck on the heads until I could be rescued. It was not fun.

The helm seat, which is a second-hand VW van seat, is

Construction of lockers under helm seat

now temporarily mounted on its box. We have chosen a seat like this because it is comfortable and has good support. It also has a pair of armrests and the capacity, as in a vehicle, to be slid forward and backward. This means that anyone at the helm can adjust the seat to their own needs. Also, in this one's case, it is rotatable and therefore can form an additional 'social' seat-

Helm seat

ing space when swivelled to face the dinette. The seat has been on the lounge table in our cottage for months and, although it was a bit of a talking point, we are glad to see it in its proper position. The

Navigation table

final height of this seat again ensures good all-round visibility for whoever is sitting there. Now that height has been determined, the steering wheel assembly and throttle/gearshift mounting structure are also fitted for convenient use of the helm. Also, at this point, Tom builds and attaches a sturdy footrest across the front of the helm area. The instrument pod is now designed and fitted, again leaving a clear view for the helm to monitor various functions on the engine control panel. At a later date, all the switches and navigation units will be mounted inside or on top of this pod.

Now that all the furniture has been constructed in ply, solid mahogany trim is fitted to the cut edges. The whole aspect of the wheelhouse is transformed from utility plywood furniture to a much more eye-catching finished product.

Meanwhile, my recovery continues apace and I am

Helm and throttle assembly, with instrument pod

strong enough to fine finish, rub down and apply varnish and/or paint to any of the pieces that can be removed from the boat and brought home, for example locker lids and the navigation instrument pod. It's wonderful to be feeling able to make a real contribution once again. I expect to be able to do a few hours each day down in the build shed very shortly. To cheer myself up I am spending vast amounts of dosh on goodies like a steering wheel, a solar panel and the very desirable electric windlass for the anchor chain.

CHAPTER FIFTEEN

The all-important galley

Plate storage – galley

Now that the wheelhouse furniture has been finished, Tom moves forward into what will be *Thea*'s galley area. This will become my pride and joy and it will be a slightly bigger galley area than we had in *Selene*. The galley and its design are very important, especially to us. All too often little thought is given to the cookery side of boat life, and the galley is rudimentary. A bit of careful design allows far more to be achieved than opening a tin of beans and warming it up in a saucepan. We will be living on board for extended periods. I love to cook and Tom loves to fish, much to the distress of the fish and shellfish populations wherever we are anchored. The idea is to have plenty of unobstructed work surfaces and storage space in what is basically a small kitchen, with all the contents. But even if you are only spending weekends on board, the ability to cook creatively is welcome.

The galley build starts off with the construction of the lock-

Forward lockers – galley

Forward lockers and recess for cooker – galley

ers, which will be underneath the work surfaces. To save a miserable job later, the interiors of these are painted out before the work surfaces go on top. They are large cave lockers that will hold various tinned and dried goods, plastic store boxes, the rubbish bin, pots and pans and – most importantly – a big crab boiling pot. The biggest cave lockers are actually deeper than Tom's arm would be able to reach into to paint, so it's pretty essential to do it now. Once afloat, we will use shallow cardboard boxes to keep the contents of these big lockers separated. This stops the lockers becoming a bit of a rummage sale, and makes it easy to draw things forward to look through when needed. Ranged around the work surface tops is storage for cooking utensils and cutlery in a set of three drawers, plus storage for various sized plates and a couple of lockers for bowls and basins. Another locker is dedicated for foodstuffs used on a daily basis, like sauces, jams and pickles. A custom mug rack is fitted holding nine mugs. We collect mugs as souvenirs on our travels and this makes for an attractive and practical display. Like most 'boat-ies' we tend to have quite a few people popping on board, so another locker provides a mug 'overflow'. Finally, some small eye-level lockers are fitted under the deck head for such things as tea towels, coffee and tea. In total we will have sixteen lockers in the galley, plus three drawers, all of which we know from past experience will be packed full!

One of the work surfaces will house a stainless steel sink with a pressurised cold water tap and a salt water faucet, powered by an electric pump. We have found that an endless supply of salt water is very handy for flushing away soapsuds, pre-washing vegetables and cleaning 'fishy' hands. All this saves precious freshwater.

Overhead lockers - galley

The cooker we have bought is a marine quality two-burner, grill and oven unit and will be fine for everything we want to do. In the early days of our married life, our cottage (which we still live in) was pretty dere-lict and we used a boat stove for about three years whilst we fitted the house out. Our new stove is set up on gimbals, which is more of a yacht thing than a motorboat thing but, trust us, motorboats still roll around. It can be distressing and dangerous to have hot pots fall off the top of the stove. Even in a tranquil anchorage, the wash from passing boats can create enough movement to be an issue.

The galley area will also be fitted with an electric extractor fan and an opening porthole. It's a lovely light bright area, mostly thanks to a fixed skylight set into the deck.

Galley rubbish can be a problem on board, and we have designed a locker for just that. A plastic box, of roughly 10-litre capacity, is attached to the inside of a dedicated locker door, which is hinged at the bottom. The locker is opened against a 'stop' and then will close under its own weight. A bi-odegradable rubbish sack can then be used to line the box and is easy to remove and take ashore for disposal.

The lockers under the sink also house the water tank connecting pipes, the stopcocks for the sink waste and the salt water faucet.

The plywood locker tops now need to have a work surface fitted to them. We spend some time choosing the right finish and eventually buy a sheet of marble-effect cream Formica, which will look just lovely against the varnished mahogany woodwork. Normally Formica is glued down with contact adhesive but we prefer to use epoxy resin to guarantee its water resistance. Lead weights, and what seems like every rock in the boatyard, are used to hold the Formica down while the glue goes off.

We are now ready to fit all the solid wood trim, after which the galley is ready for me to start the never-ending job of filling, painting and varnishing.

Locker for rubbish bin

And now we have most of our galley in place. I am back on the staff full time and we go back to our 'Team Owen' build cycle – Tom doing the building and me doing the finishing. As we move into the early spring, we are starting to see light at the end of the tunnel.

Galley

CHAPTER SIXTEEN

The even more important heads

Lockers in the heads

In which…

- **The galley sole goes down**
- **The heads are finished**

LATE APRIL 2016
LAUNCH DAY MINUS
SEVEN AND A HALF MONTHS

To make life easier for working in *Thea*'s galley area, the next job is to fit the galley sole. Before this can be done a stack of four lockers have to be built on the starboard side, which the cabin sole will sit up against. The sole is fitted in three moveable sections so any one or all of them can be lifted for access to the bilge. It's very nice to be able to stand on a proper 'floor' instead of slipping and sliding around on the sloping sides of the hull, particularly for me with my still slightly weak legs.

Our next job is to build the steps leading from the wheelhouse down to the galley, which will include the housing for the fridge. The addition of these steps remarkably improves the ease and safety of access to the area that we are currently working in. The lovely electric fridge I bought some months ago will be fitted later under these steps, so Tom builds in plenty of ventilation for the unit as it will produce an amount of heat that will need to be dissipated. From our past experience with compressor-operated marine fridges, we know that they tend to run for about a quarter of an hour every hour to maintain their temperature. However, the fridge we have chosen actually performs much better than this, only cutting in two or three times per twenty-four hours.

Personnel lockers

The next move is to fit-out the heads (toilet) compartment. We know exactly what we want. The dimensions of the heads have been worked out to give maximum room for washing and dressing within the confines of space available. Lockers are built in, and the work surface is finished with the same Formica that we used in the galley, keeping everything light, bright and easy to clean. We will be fitting a GRP sink, but it can't go in yet because it hasn't arrived. The supplier has come up with a myriad of excuses for the delay, including the surmise that it must have been stolen by the courier. Never mind, it will arrive eventually and will go in the space provided together with its pressurised cold water tap. We are not fitting a calorifier hot water system as it seems a little pointless to us to run the main engine merely to produce hot water. We have always been perfectly content with a hot water supply provided by a kettle and, as we typically cruise on our own, we don't have to worry about other people's preferences. Similarly, we do not intend to fit a shower as we both find the dampness they produce in a heads compartment, and the amount of water they use, to be unacceptable. We grew up in an age

Fridge locker and steps

Heads on its plinth

when an all-over wash every day was standard practice, and that's fine with us. We'd rather have the treat of going ashore to a yacht club to use better shower facilities or, if the weather is fine, we can use a solar shower in the cockpit.

The sea toilet is installed and sea cocks are fitted, though no pipework is added at this point to make painting easier. Natural light and ventilation are provided by an opening porthole and a ventilator fitted on the deck. Finally, the sole, trim and a door are fitted, which more or less completes the heads for the moment.

Our workshop tools, and in particular the electric drills, sanders and planes, are getting some very hard use. Most of Tom's electric tools have built more than one boat and we are constantly 'touching wood' (not difficult in the work shed) that they will soldier on until the end of this project. Sadly, his much loved but very ancient Black & Decker drill decides that it's had enough and explodes in spectacular fashion. There is a belch of black smoke, followed by flames. Tom quickly unplugs it and throws it out of the shed to burn itself out. It's definitely not repairable.

More rubbing down

Meantime I have my ongoing task of rubbing down, painting and varnishing. Some of the lockers on board the boat, particularly in the wheelhouse, are vast and require some gymnastics to reach into. It's only three months since my hip replacement and my surgeon can't decide whether to be pleased or appalled by some of the contortions that I send him pictures of.

Crouching on the ground to take the 'skin' off a tin of bilge paint, fortunately when off the boat, I drop it. The tin stays upright but the paint shoots over a metre in the air, describes a perfect parabola, and then lands on my head. Half my face and most of my hair are an attractive shade of blue, the paint dripping with a beguiling slurp onto the ground. I hope for some Mrs Braveheart analogies, but Mrs Smurf is the most popular vote! Half a bottle of thinners does little for the condition of my hair, but at least I'm back to a mostly redhead.

Our home is still filled with a multitude of bits of woodwork in various stages of finish and they cover beds, tables and chairs. It's a good thing our friends don't mind eating on their lap when they visit for dinner.

It's lovely to have the heads compartment construction mostly finished and Tom is ready to move on to the final section of our accommodation – the fore cabin – our bedroom.

CHAPTER SEVENTEEN

Our cosy cabin

Porthole – fore cabin

In which…

- **The fore cabin is built**
- **Varnish starts to go on the furniture in the wheelhouse**
- **'Finishing' work starts on the foredeck**

EARLY MAY 2016
LAUNCH DAY MINUS SEVEN MONTHS

The last but not the least section of *Thea*'s accommodation is the fore cabin – our 'nest'. Eventually this will contain an offset double bunk with big storage bins underneath, and a selection of smaller personnel lockers under and alongside it. There will be four portholes, two opening and two fixed, and a large opening hatch leading to the foredeck. But first, several semi-bulk-heads and a chain locker bulkhead have to be fitted. These will reinforce the forepart of the hull below the water line. The plywood pieces that will form the top of the bunk are shaped and fitted on top of these bulkheads, with two access hatches to the storage bins underneath. All of this work is fairly straightforward, and we end up with a well-supported hull. The rest of the furniture is a little more time con-suming and fiddly, but eventually eight small and two large lockers have been assembled. The forward locker under the bunk will house the controls for the electric anchor winch on the foredeck.

Tom then double skins the inside of the hull around the top of the bunk to provide extra insulation. This will protect us from condensation and keep our bedding dry. Four holes are cut for portholes and reinforced with a plywood ring on the inside. The portholes we have bought have been designed to fit a nominally 1-inch thick hull and this extra ring will give us that required thickness. They are another unusual extravagance for us. We fitted similar ones in *Selene* and, even then, they cost a week's salary each. A company called Daveys in London provide a range of classic boat hardware, in-cluding these lovely solid bronze portholes.

Fore cabin bunk construction underway

Anchor locker

Fore cabin bunk top and lockers

Due to the hull form the fore cabin has a raised cabin sole, which gives only sitting headroom by the bunk. This is no great problem as it is purely a sleeping cabin and full standing headroom is not important.

Tom's work in the fore cabin takes some time so I amuse myself applying three of what will be five coats of varnish to the furniture in the wheelhouse. I'm leaving the last two coats until work has been completed that might cause damage to the final finish. We shall be moving on to work on the foredeck shortly and, in preparation, I apply the epoxy filler to the join between the deck and the toe rail, rubbing it down to produce a radius. Tom had already doubled up the ply, increasing the thickness of the toe rail to an inch. Whilst I'm up there I use more epoxy filler to fair all of the recessed screw heads and then sand down the deck.

The construction of our inside furniture is more or less finished, and we can get an idea of how good our living space will be.

We've been pretty single-minded during the build, but I have the opportunity to go to a Rod Stewart concert with Michèle, and that's not something that an aging rock chick can turn down. I shower off the day's labours in the boatyard facilities, put on some slap and am well ready when my chum arrives to pick me up. I'm a bit creaky yet, but we have a whale of a time – the man can still strut his stuff and it is definitely worth taking the evening off.

Fore cabin porthole and personnel locker

Dinette with first coats of paint and varnish

CHAPTER EIGHTEEN

Better weather – back to the outside

Stanchion base

In which…

- **The decks are sheathed**
- **Mounts are fitted for deck fittings**
- **The fore hatch is made**
- **The rubbing piece, toe rail and cockpit capping pieces are fitted**

We've been waiting for the temperature to improve so that we can resume work on the outside of the boat and get on with all the jobs that the winter stopped us doing. I have already used epoxy filler to fair the recessed screw heads and sanded down the deck, and now we start the job of sheathing all the decks, including the wheelhouse roof, with glass fibre cloth and epoxy resin. This doesn't take as long as we expected and that is a bit of a soul-lifter as many jobs have taken much longer than anticipated. These deck areas are worth sheathing to protect them from the abrasion of the chain, the anchor and anything else heavy and/or sharp. Once the sheathing has been completed, it is sanded to remove any roughness and coated with a couple of layers of epoxy resin. This produces a glass-like surface that, until it is buffed down, is quite difficult to retain a footing on, particularly on the wheelhouse roof which has no toe rail to stop you falling off! Slipping would pretty well ensure a trip to hospital as it is many feet down to the ground.

Two long and substantial iroko handrails go onto the wheelhouse roof. Almost immediately these make their presence felt as it becomes easier to move along the side decks with something to hold onto, and we also feel less vulnerable on the wheelhouse roof with the handrails between us and infinity.

Now is the time to fit a variety of plywood or solid timber pads where, eventually, various deck fittings will be mounted, for example ventilators, naviga-

Sheathing wheelhouse roof

tion lights, solar panel, cleats, stanchion bases and hatches. All of these pads are radiused and epoxied.

At this stage, a heavy oak plank is fitted on the bow ready to have the anchor windlass, pulpit and bow roller attached.

The fore hatch coamings are assembled around the deck aperture that has been cut to take them. The hatch itself, once built, is removed to be painted separately.

Port samson post - stern deck

Two extra jobs can now be undertaken – the rubbing pieces for the hull and the toe rails. First, we make and fit two iroko rubbing pieces. These are made of 4 x 1-inch planks, scarfed together, with a cove line running down the middle and heavily radiused top and bottom. We fit these dry, screwing them into place, and then remove them to coat the mating surfaces with epoxy ready to reattach them for the final time. Though the assembled length of timber is some 32 feet long and takes some handling, it is fairly easy to get a fair curve around the hull. This is quite important as any irregularities will be

Wheelhouse roof with handrails and solar panel framing

blindingly obvious once coats of dark hull paint have been applied and the cove line has been picked out in bright yellow. The rubbing piece also covers the hull joint where the plywood of the raised foredeck meets the hull proper. It sits on top of the stringer/deck shelf on the inside of the hull to which it is screwed, thus producing a heavily reinforced area of the hull at what could be a vul-

Pulpit

Fore hatch coaming

nerable spot for impact.

The next task is to attach the iroko capping pieces. These fit around the top of the toe rails and are more pieces of woodwork that will attract the eye as they will be varnished in contrast to the dark hull and the cream deck. Two radiused sections are fitted to the toe rails on the two quarters of the stern. These are aesthetically pleasing and again smooth the lines around the back of the cockpit.

Our final job is to fit more iroko capping pieces, this time around the cockpit coaming, repeating the radiused corners and complementing the pleasing lines of the toe rail.

We consider this to be the last structural job and are looking forward to doing some cosmetics.

Rubbing piece

Corner pieces for capping and toe rails

Ouch – the price of teak!

Teak laid cockpit

LATE JULY 2016
LAUNCH DAY MINUS
FOUR AND A HALF MONTHS

Roughly six months after the Christmas glazing disaster when all the epoxy went opaque, we finally get around to fitting the glass in the wheelhouse. The outside glazing bars are re-epoxied and the laminated glass is bedded into Sikaflex. Then it is secured with the second set of glazing bars, which are pinned and Sikaflexed into place. Little crosses of masking tape go onto the glass, as we are in the habit of popping our heads through the window spaces to have a chat. The wheelhouse now feels like it genuinely has an inside and outside. The addition of the radiused corner pieces softens

Glazed windows

the 'squareness' of the windows. This is a small touch that adds to the labour of fitting the glass but is worth the effort to achieve the visual effect we want.

We have decided that installing insulation on *Thea*'s deck heads throughout the accommodation is a good idea. The advantages are that it stops the heat of summer turning the interior into a greenhouse and equally

Wiring tails

stops any heat generated in the boat from leaving through the deck in the winter. Incidentally, it will combat the formation of condensation, which is often a problem on boats and leads to the growth of mould. The insulation, which is 12 mm thick closed cell rigid foam commonly used in the building trade, will be finished with a covering of 6 mm ply. This will be painted magnolia or, as we now know it, orchid, and will create an attractive deck head highlighted by the varnished mahogany beams.

The wiring harness for interior and exterior lighting, aerials and electronics is fitted in channels cut into the insulation. Once this has been done, the plywood is pinned into place, with tails of electric cable fed through ready to be connected to lights and instruments. We are always slightly surprised by the amount of cable required to do a job like this – enough to go round the boat several times and, it seems, halfway to France. As the lengths of cable are fitted pieces of masking tape are attached to each end, onto which we write the designated function of each individual cable. This saves a lot of time-wasting and irritation later, trying to identify which cable does what.

For Tom, the next move is to construct a laid teak deck, followed by the seats in the cockpit. Four figures worth of teak has been delivered and slowly but surely this is cut into the appropriate patterns and glued down with epoxy resin. Four hatches are also made and laid with teak – three for the cockpit seats and one as an access hatch in the cockpit sole. The teak decking is finished off by filling the rebates with decking-quality Sikaflex and then sanding everything smooth. The end product, though expensive, is glorious. The cockpit, as it is quite large, forms an impressive feature and we are glad that we made the investment in a laid teak finish. We know, of course, that it will never look this good again as we intend to let it weather to silver, but that is perfectly acceptable to us.

Meantime I am covered in dust, again. I put three coats of epoxy on the rubbing piece, the capping pieces and the solid wood of the wheelhouse and rub them down carefully but with enthusiasm between coats. In the 35°C plus heat, it's been a challenge. We've got a good result though and it is now ready for the application of paint and varnish.

An incidental job, amongst all of this, has been the fitting of the missing sinks. Our lovely and long-awaited cream GRP sink for the heads has now arrived and is fitted in the work surface.

First piece of laid teak decking

Epoxy-coated stern deck

Then we lay some marine-themed tiles around the back of the basin as a splash back. The tiles we choose are another unusual extravagance for us, and include feature tiles with figured shellfish, but we are delighted with the result. The second sink, a deep square stainless steel model that took us some time to track down, now goes into the work surface in the galley.

At home in the evenings we have been trying to find 'off the shelf' davits to fit on the stern deck for carrying our dinghy. There is nothing available that meets our needs so, once again, Tom takes to his drawing board to sketch out an appropriate design. They need to be capable of being swivelled out of

Heads sink and tiling

Galley sink

the way or removed entirely, and strong enough to carry a dinghy with its outboard in a seaway. The completed plans go to our stainless fabricators and we look forward to seeing them in three dimensions.

We are now ready to apply some paint and varnish, and to fit very shiny expensive things – how exciting.

CHAPTER TWENTY

Paint, plumbing and squashy things

Feature tile in heads

AUGUST 2016
LAUNCH DAY MINUS FOUR MONTHS

While Tom has been busy laying the teak in the cockpit, I have been occupied applying cream paint to the foredeck, side decks and wheelhouse roof. The apparent colour of this paint has been a bit of a concern. Visitors to the work shed have been asking us why we are painting *Thea* yellow, calling us the 'banana boat'! It is with some considerable relief that we realise that the locker lids and hatches being painted out in the open air look reassuringly cream – it appears that something about the plastic sheeting of our shed roof is distorting the appearance of the colour of paintwork inside.

Tom now starts to attach the many, many deck fittings that will sit on top of the mounting pads, such as the anchor winch, cleats, stanchion bases, bollards and a fairly hefty two-speed self-tailing winch. The latter is fitted on the stern deck in case we need extra muscle to handle stern or kedge anchor warps. While Tom is doing this work, I move in and complete the cream paintwork throughout the cockpit.

The list of finishing off jobs seems endless and it feels like every item ticked off our list produces the addition of two more. Maybe the light we could see at the end of the tunnel was a man with a torch bringing more work.

We will soon move onto the plumbing, wiring and electronics, but first two tables need to be built – one for the wheelhouse and one removable one for alfresco dining in the cockpit. I then have the challenge of obtaining a mirror-like varnish finish on them to complement the quality of Tom's joinery.

The fore hatch is fitted to its

Dinette table

Starboard side of wheelhouse

Completed cockpit

coamings on the foredeck, then it and the skylight for the galley are both 'double glazed' with an additional sheet of Perspex to give an air gap. This, once again, stops condensation forming on them and dripping inside the boat.

I am now inside the boat applying the last of the five coats of varnish to all the solid timber and the furniture. As a reward I can then paint out any remaining lockers, and the headlining between the beams. The finished effect, we think, is breathtaking.

Tom starts on the plumbing for the freshwater system. This is reasonably complicated as we have to link up both of our tanks so that they can be used individually. It includes fitting a sight-gauge to each tank so that we can monitor the levels. A filter unit, pump and accumulator also have to be accommodated in the plumbing. Most of these bits and pieces end up being fitted in one of the lockers in the heads.

In addition, he is fitting the pipework for both our bilge pumps – one is a large capacity electric unit of 2,000 gph and the second is a manual pump of 25 gpm. Hopefully neither will ever be used. Having them is like carrying an umbrella – it always stops the rain (or, in this case, the leak).

I've spent some considerable time worrying about the issue of the soft furnishings. I don't think I have the skill to make them up myself, but we don't want to spend a small fortune paying someone else to do it. A

Foredeck showing forward hatch and skylight over galley

compromise is finding the material ourselves online and then employing a local upholster to make up the various cushions throughout the boat. We are delighted to find some material that appears to be a close match for the fabric we loved on *Selene*. It's a very traditional pattern and colour – a deep red with gold fleur-de-lys – which most certainly matches the style of the boat.

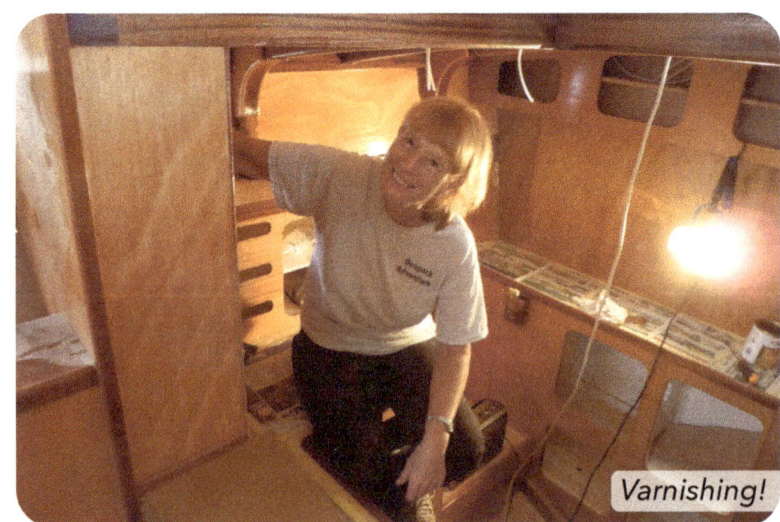
Varnishing!

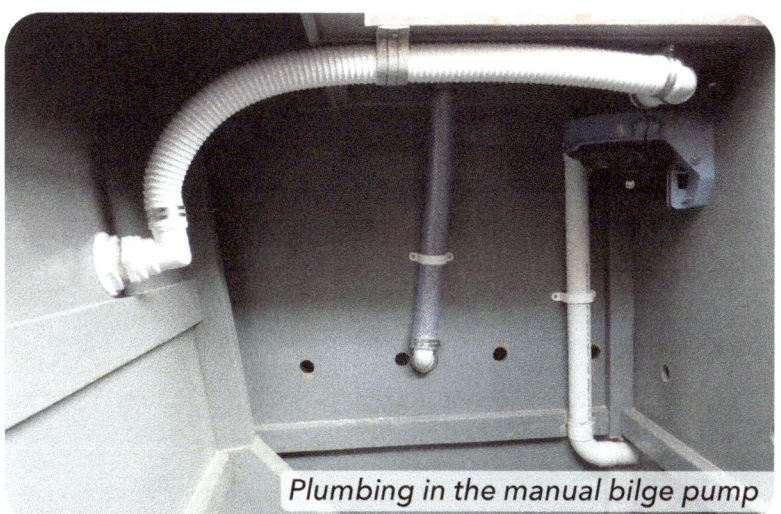

Plumbing in the manual bilge pump

Thea is becoming more complete by the day. The next job will be painting the hull.

Soft furnishings in dinette

Bronze on blue

Propellor

In which…

- **The hull is painted**
- **The portholes go in**
- **The decks are coated with deck paint**

SEPTEMBER-OCTOBER 2016
LAUNCH DAY MINUS THREE MONTHS

Finishing and painting *Thea*'s hull is the next job on the list. Many years ago, when *Selene* was only a twinkle in Tom's eye, we saw one of the yachts used by the students at Dartmouth Naval College sailing slowly upriver. She was dark, dark blue, with plenty of varnish work and a gold trim along her rubbing piece. We were stunned and immediately agreed that that was the colour scheme we would choose for any future boat. It worked brilliantly on *Selene*, and we've always known that we want *Thea* to be the same. We spend many happy hours – no, honestly – filling and rubbing down large and small imperfections on the hull surface. This is one of the jobs that we have to be patient about as the gloss paint will be very unforgiving. Once we've achieved what looks

Fine filling the hull

like a reasonable finish, the hull is treated to a coat of two pack high build primer. This is a medium blue colour and over a couple of days we sand most of it off again, covering everything in the work shed, including ourselves, with a thin patina of blue dust. Facemasks are obviously essential! The hull transforms from a rather smart medium blue to a rather patchy mess. However, the high build primer has done its job and we now have a fair surface upon which to apply the finishing coats of dark blue. This is a single pack mono-urethane paint, not a two pack. We know from experience that fenders and other boats will scuff any paint finish within days of being afloat and we want a finish we can touch in easily.

High build filler coat

Sanding the filler

Our paint supplier has given us a highly recommended laying off brush as a gift. Tom rolls on the gloss paint and then I lay it off with the brush provided. We are overwhelmed by the mirror-like finish. Everything in the workshop, including ourselves, is reflected back at us. This is a fair and just reward for hours and hours of preparation.

Our six very expensive bronze portholes are now fitted and provide a stunning contrast to the dark blue hull.

The boot top and the antifouling are painted on by Tom, who then cuts in the bright yellow cove lines on the rubbing pieces. I am allowed the honour of pulling off the masking tape so we can see the effect of the completed exterior paint job. Pulling off the masking tape is definitely

Mirror finish

the best part of painting – all of the joy with none of the labour.

Meantime, I finish the varnishing of the toe rail and then cover the working areas of the deck that have not been painted cream with non-slip light grey deck paint.

For a finishing touch to the hull, white decals reading 'THEA – Dartmouth' are very carefully attached to the transom.

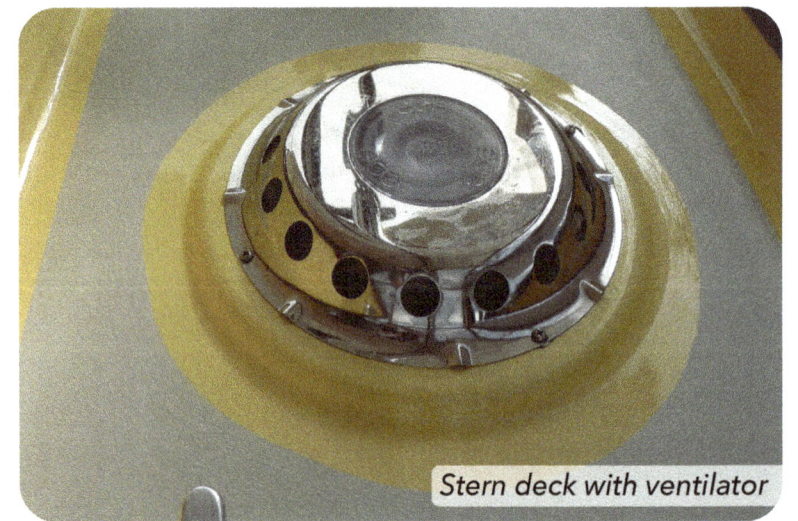

Stern deck with ventilator

Propeller and rudder

All our coats of unctions are now complete, and we can attach our lovely bronze propeller. Then we take down the sheets that are shrouding the work shed. Finally, we can step back far enough to see our finished handiwork, albeit through the slightly opaque plastic sheeting. But we can see enough to be thrilled.

Stern decals, davits, boot top and antifouling

CHAPTER TWENTY-TWO

Thea passes with flying colours

Out she comes

In which...

- **The final fitting of electrics, gas system and engine takes place**
- **The gas and engine installations are signed off**
- **The in-build sign off and valuation survey report are issued**
- **The pre-launch checks are completed for ballast and engine**
- **The mast and rigging are fitted**
- **The carpet is laid**

NOVEMBER 2016
LAUNCH DAY MINUS ONE MONTH

With the cosmetics finished, it's now time to connect up the wiring loom to assorted lights, electronics and pumps. This all proves fairly straightforward thanks to the name tags we attached to the wires when they were tracked through the deck head. Our blown hot air system is wired in and tested, and all is well.

Finally the 250 watt solar panel that we've set up on the wheelhouse roof is connected and, even though the boat is still inside the shed, the panel starts feeding a useful number of amps into the battery system. The solar panel is fitted with an 'intelligent' control box, which boosts battery charging. This bit of kit was quite expensive, but it is definitely worth it. The actual input is monitored by an ammeter fitted in the circuit. Even on an overcast day we can be pretty sure of getting between 2.5 and 4 amps per hour during daylight hours. This input will safely cover the day-to-day electrical needs of the boat while we are living on board, without any need to run the main engine. LED bulbs have been fitted for domestic lighting. The range of these bulbs now available means that we can have the equivalent of a 35 watt bulb in a lamp that only uses 3 watts. Thus the various cabins are very well illuminated indeed. We do have some power-hungry items on board – the fridge, the heater, and the charging circuits for the laptop and tablet – but the input from the solar panel will be more than adequate to cover their needs. Nowadays there is no limit to the number of electrical appliances that can be bought to be fitted on board – to the point that some vessels can only function if they are connected to the power circuit of a marina or run a generator. As we are anticipating travelling and need to be self-sufficient, we've kept such items to a minimum.

Tom has fitted the gas system, taking the advice of our local gas engineer, who now visits to test the system and issue a Gas Compliance certificate.

The fuel lines for the engine are fitted, plus other odds and ends for the engine installation. Our local Beta engineer makes his site visit to sign off the installation as required for our engine warranty.

Probably the most important visit is from our surveyor who happily issues our in-build sign off and valuation survey report, enabling us to get *Thea*'s insurance. With a 'one-off' build, it is important to establish a pedigree for a boat, both for insurance and for re-sale value.

Arrival of the ballast

We now feel confident to send out invitations to *Thea*'s launch ceremony in a month's time. Incidentally, I have an appointment to see my orthopaedic

Success!

surgeon, who books me in for the replacement of my second hip the day after the launch ceremony – what timing!

During this month we have *Thea* hauled out of the shed and briefly launched to give us the opportunity to fit the internal ballast. This will ensure that she floats nicely on her lines when we have our public launch. We decide to do this because we found the launch of our previous boat *Selene* very stressful indeed, as we had no absolute idea where she would float. As it happened all was well, but any errors would have been a very public embarrassment. We load 6 cwt of concrete blocks into *Thea*'s bilge and secure them with straps to the ballast beds already constructed. We have chosen to use concrete blocks because they are cheap, and they won't rust. Individual blocks weigh about 44 lb each and it's relatively easy to put them on board whilst *Thea* is alongside the pontoon, and then transfer them to their position in the bilge. That done, we fire up the engine and make sure all is well. There is no unforeseen vibration and the sound insulation, as anticipated, does a sterling job. We are able to hold a conversation across the wheelhouse at normal volume. It's really good to know that all of our efforts to sound-proof the engine have been so successful. This is also the time to check for any odd leaks both in the hull and around the engine – not that we are expecting any, but you never know. We are completely watertight – another tick on the list.

Once this is done, we are hauled out again ready to have the mast and rigging fitted. The mast is a section cut out of a damaged mast and is some 15 feet long. Tom has fitted the various pieces of equipment to it, tracking the wiring down the inside. To help maintenance, mast steps are fitted for easy access to the top of the mast. It has been lying around the workshop for some weeks, as we obviously couldn't fit it to the boat whilst we were in the shed. A local rigger turns up, works out the length of the mast stays, and fits them. All we have to do then is link the electric cables coming from the mast to a junction box underneath the deck in the galley. These are all fed through a watertight wiring gland on the deck by the mast step. We now have a working VHF, wind speed and direction instrument, spreader light and steaming light.

A final job is to fit carpet throughout the accommodation. We look around for something that has a built-in fabric underlay, which will add to our already impressive sound insulation. We find an acceptable carpet that is stain and bleach resistant in a suitably forgiving speckled fawn colour. Apart from the normal possible boat spillages, we travel with our cat Buddy, who is very reliable with his habits but is prone to bringing up hairballs, as cats do. Indeed, we travel with a small herb garden planted in a washing up bowl and it includes some ordinary grass for this very purpose.

Mast in situ

And we're done – all ready for the big day.

CHAPTER TWENTY-THREE

Finally – the big day

Afloat at last

DECEMBER 2016
LAUNCH DAY!

Our chosen launch date falls in early December. Not really the best time for such things and the day dawns grey, damp and pretty cold. However, our friends are made of sterling stuff and we have a crowd of over a hundred to celebrate the day with us.

We do at least have some cover within our boat shed, and the yard staff, helpful as always, have scrubbed down and transported some picnic tables and chairs ready for the buffet we have laid out. Kind chums have contributed to the supply of goodies – even a tea urn appears. My lovely 'niece-in-law' Katharine and my nephew Andrew have created wonderful launch cakes to help with the celebrations.

Throughout our project, the management and staff at Premier Marina, Noss on Dart, have been consistently helpful and supportive. The CEO, Peter Bradshaw, has visited us on a number of occasions to offer encouragement and congratulations. The management team provides a case of fizz as their contribution to the celebrations and we are delighted to see so many of the staff turn up for the event, even those who are not on duty.

Kym naming Thea

My sister-in-law, Kym, performs the 'naming' ceremony, which continues a family tradition. My mother Marjorie, sadly no longer with us, 'named' *Selene* over twenty years ago.

As always with celebrations, the day flashes by and we don't have a chance to speak to everybody at length. Quite a lot of the day is spent organising tours around *Thea* once she is in the water – this is Tom's province, and making sure that people have enough to eat and drink – this is my remit, ably assisted as always by Michèle and Paul.

The crowd assembles

What we do know is that it is a very happy day. We are proud of our achievement but humbled by the genuine affection and regard of the friends and family who have joined us.

The party

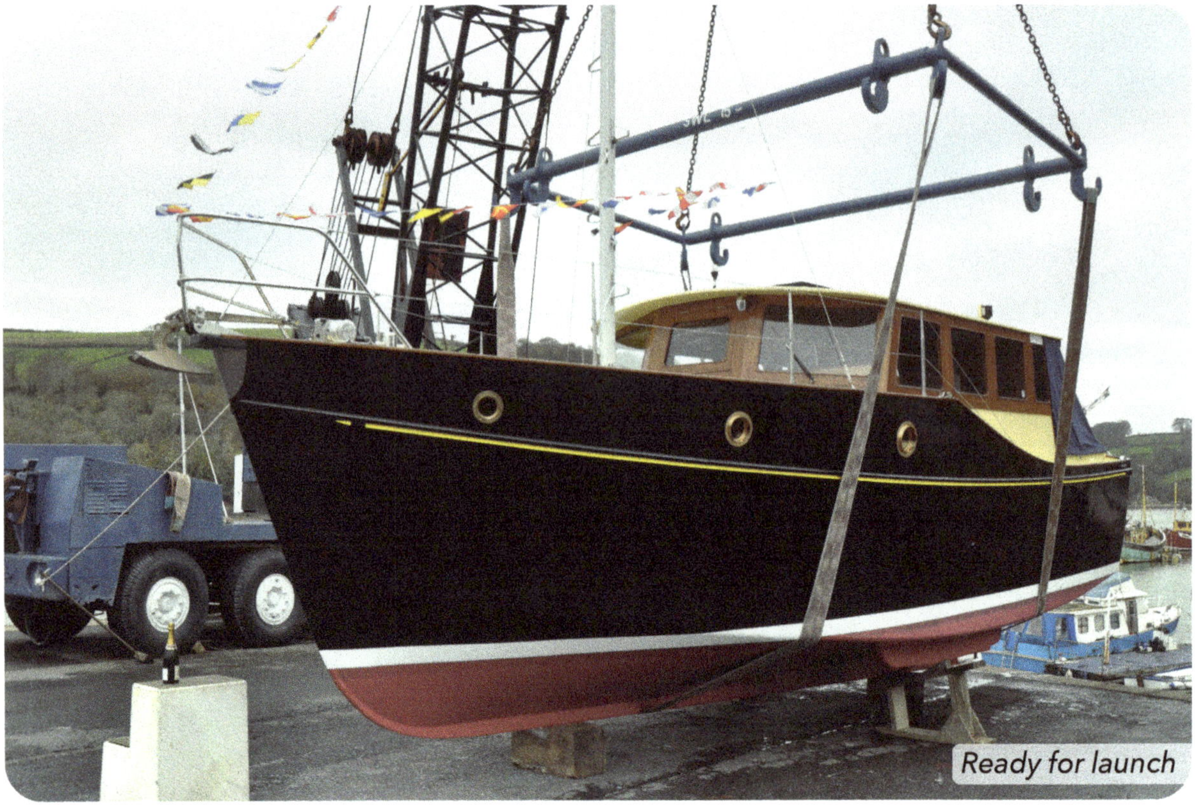

Ready for launch

Hurrah!

MAR '15

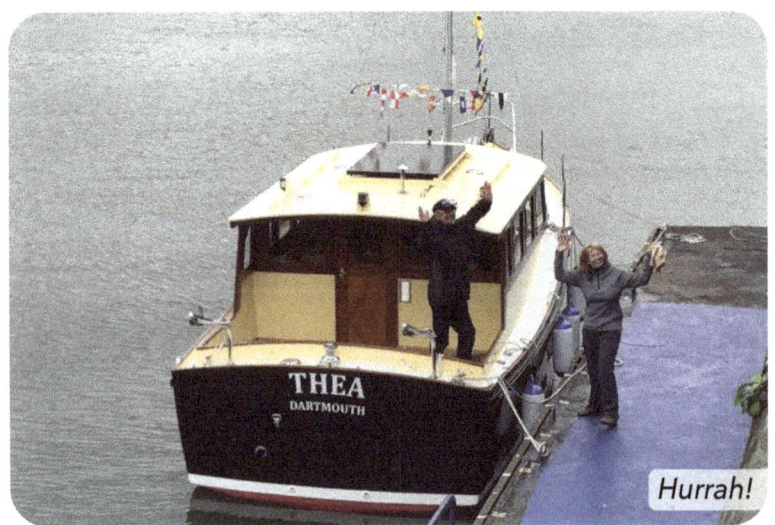

There must be a begynnyng of any great matter,
but the contenewing unto the end untyll it be thoroughly ffynyshed
yeldes the trew glory.

—Sir Francis Drake

That which kept us going

Without doubt the boat build was a long hard slog, and there were many things we relied on to keep our spirits up. We were working 12-hour days, 7 days a week, so it would have been easy to get discouraged and lose momentum. Whilst we had a goal that was of great importance to us both, we needed small treats, encouragement and light-hearted moments to see us through.

For example, domestically, having access to our 'canteen' meant that we could have coffee/tea breaks with others in the yard, supplemented by a well-stocked cookie jar, and swap 'boaty' stories. We were careful to keep these breaks under some control as talking about boats can lead to protracted conversations that last throughout the morning and into the afternoon! Fine if you've got nothing else to do…

We decided to make our food breaks something to look forward to. I cooked bacon and eggs at home to make our breakfast sandwiches, and we took them down to the shed wrapped in foil. We always started work early in the morning and these hot butties, with a steaming cup of coffee, were an excellent way to start the day. Our breakfast break gave us the opportunity to sort out our jobs for the day and get everything clear and understood before we started work. Starting work early in the morning also meant that we could avoid the chaotic school run down the narrow lane leading out of our village – not a journey for the faint-hearted. Lunch, certainly in the winter, was often something I'd thrown into the slow cooker in the morning and then left bubbling away until lunchtime.

Boatyard wraps

Sometimes it was difficult to concentrate with the luscious smells coming from the 'canteen', but lunch was definitely something to look forward to and so much better than a cold sandwich. A late afternoon treat might be a salad wrap. A well-filled wrap can be a difficult thing to eat on a building site, but I came up with the idea of clipping a bag-closer across the end – ideal!

We were determined not to repeat the mistake we made in *Selene*'s build – having very comfy chairs – but we did manage to salvage some plastic garden chairs from the local recycling centre. This gave us somewhere basic to sit ourselves and something to offer to chums when they came to see us.

Our wonderful friends not only tolerated our absence but were always ready to lend a helping hand. Their visits were a treat – especially when they brought doughnuts or cake! And sometimes a whole lunch! Some visitors travelled a considerable distance to reach us and we were touched by their support. They all accepted the paint-/resin-encrusted chairs and the wonky table, and their smiley faces and encouragement kept us going (the cake helped, of course).

Lunch

Little things kept us amused, especially the regular visits we had from a variety of animals and insects. It soon became apparent that we were getting four-legged nocturnal visitors who left mysterious footprints in the dust that accumulated on different surfaces inside the shed, and in the mud outside – we think that we had a visiting stoat or possibly polecat, and outside we most definitely had a foraging hedgehog. During the summer we had a bit of an invasion of

Lunch

flies, attracted to the heat between our 'sheets' and the polythene roof. They were quickly followed by a succession of insect-eating birds who swooped in through the opening window and took the flies on the wing. We were visited by at least two very large crickets, who were glorious to look at. Crumbs we dropped at mealtimes were picked up by transient field mice. And Fran, our boat neighbour, had a lovely dog called Lara. She kept herself and us well exercised chasing the innumerable balls we threw for her.

Throughout the build, as *Thea* blossomed, we grew stronger and leaner, though our bank balance grew weaker. Although we had health issues we had to overcome, generally the work was an excellent form of exercise, both mentally and physically. I'm sure I wouldn't have recovered from my hip oper-

Lunch

ation so quickly – regaining my agility in a very few weeks – without the need to clamber on and off of the boat every few minutes and, amongst other things, folding myself into lockers on a very regular basis to sand, paint and varnish.

Boat jumbles provided small opportunities to take a break from our routine, but we tried to keep 'time out' to a minimum, partly because we wanted *Thea* finished and on the water, and partly because we were paying monthly ground rent and didn't want to go over budget.

During my unplanned period of 'down-time' we were careful to keep me feeling involved. At the beginning and end of the day we would review progress, and I would ring Tom during the day to catch

Coffee break

Footprints in the dust

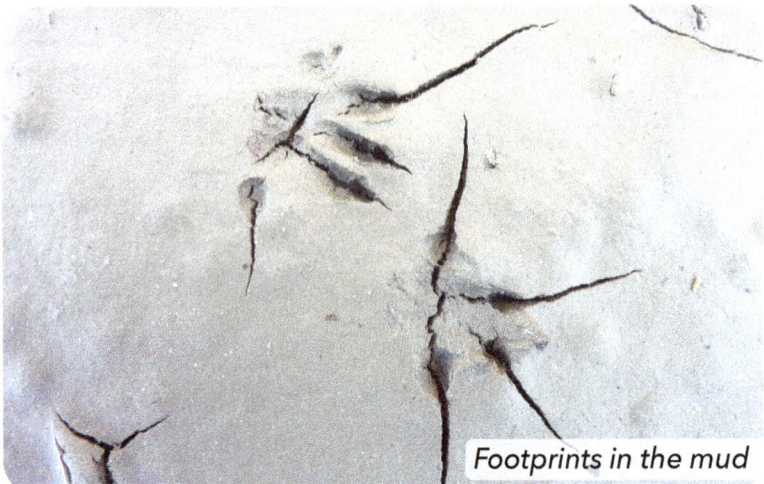

Footprints in the mud

Cricket

up on the day's doings and see if any problems needed talking through. He also took plenty of photographs of work in progress that we could study each evening. We were lucky that I was well supported by friends at home, so Tom was able to continue with the project knowing that I would be OK. Of course, searching on the Internet kept me occupied for a chunk of time. We remembered that, when we built *Selene*, the Internet was something that wasn't available to most people in their home, and certainly not to us. Consequently, we had to spend weeks searching through telephone directories and yachting periodicals, days on the telephone and long frustrating hours on the road looking for suppliers of necessary equipment. Nowadays a few minutes will normally find an answer and get the answer shipped to you at the best price.

These may seem small things, but they added to our sense of wellbeing during what could have been a stressful and difficult time.

Afterword

Was the 18 months the project took worth it?

In total *Thea* represents over 9,000 'person' hours of work. From our point of view, she was most definitely worth the effort. We have created a boat that is 'custom built' by us, for us. We could never have afforded a brand-new boat off the shelf and, even if we could, Tom would have spent probably years altering it to suit what he wanted (if that was even possible!).

We know that we are lucky to have had the time, the finance and the skill to see it through. Boatyards always have unfinished or abandoned projects lying in corners. We didn't want that to be us, and so we were pretty single-minded in our approach. It helped that we work well as a team, offering each other practical and emotional support. This was particularly important when I was in a great deal of pain with my hip, and Tom was cold, damp and tired in the boat shed.

We knew that this was going to be the last project of this size that we would undertake, and we were pretty chuffed that – in our pensionable years – we saw it through and came out with a top result.

The Premier Marinas media team publicised the build and launch of *Thea* and we were later approached by the marine press regarding an article about her build. This proved to be successful and, from her launch onward, *Thea* has been the subject of critical acclaim and has been featured in a number of pieces in boating magazines.

Three seasons on – does *Thea* work for us?

Over the last three summers *Thea* has carried us some 1,500 miles and we can safely say that she has achieved all of the goals we set ourselves.

One of our primary objectives was all-round visibility from the wheelhouse – our 'lounge/diner'. Once cruising it took many months to stop ourselves waking at the crack of dawn and rushing up to the dinette berth, excited by the thought of taking our coffee in the warmth and comfort of our saloon, wrapped in our fleecy blankets and able to watch the world go by. As things come to life on the water there is so much to see, be it boatmen taking out their potting boats or flights of seabirds beat-

Wheelhouse

Fore cabin

Helm

Galley

Heads

ing up on a shoal of fry. Whatever the weather, there is always something happening out there when you are afloat, and now we can be a part of it. For instance, we tend to notice a lost dinghy drifting past before anyone else – sometimes even before its owner. It does mean flying around like International Rescue on occasions, but that's part of the deal on the water.

Our accommodation works perfectly for us. We were sure it would, after all we spent a long time mulling it over at the design stage. But the reality is just wonderful, and we cruise in perfect comfort.

We certainly don't miss being wet and cold underway, fighting with reluctant sails, trying to control wet sheets, heaving on winches and having sun/salt blisters for the first weeks of the season. We now travel from port to port in comfort, maybe even with the heater on. Sea state allowing, we can get underway regardless of other weather conditions. The direction of the wind no longer matters, neither does the rain or the cold.

With respect to the use of fuel, sailing purists may not use their engines but owners of cruising sailboats boats tend to, and certainly we did. Consequently, the cost of diesel over the season is little more for us now than it was when we had a sailboat.

The shallow draft is a joy, not only because we can explore little-known creeks and harbours, but also because we tend to be the closest boat to the shore when we are on anchor! I don't miss nights spent on the outside edge of a crowded anchorage worrying because other boats might drag onto us in the dark.

We have a large uncluttered cockpit – no wheel, no rigging, no bits of rope – good for those who like to fish as well as those who like to socialise! *Thea* has proved to be a stable fishing platform – as anticipated the chine build dampens any roll.

Something that comes as a pleasant surprise is our clean passage through the water. The hull doesn't create much of a bow wave and there is little disturbance at the transom. It's nice not to leave walls of broken water in your wake.

If I had to identify two things I miss about sail, the first would be the ability to take on the challenge of really heavy weather. We had intended to take *Thea* to Ireland in the summer of 2018 but, some

Thea in action

10 miles out from the Isles of Scilly, we were beaten back by a big Atlantic swell meeting an unforecast moderate easterly wind. These were not conditions that would have stopped us in *Selene*, in whom we made that crossing many times, but we were not prepared to endure a 26-hour beating in our relatively small motorboat. The second issue is the lack of another form of propulsion if the prop becomes fouled. We hope to have reduced the possibility of this problem by fitting a rope cutter, but this won't help with the increasing amount of discarded net and large sheets of plastic that float around the coast. We'll just have to travel hopefully.

We will never forget the very memorable sails we've had over the years but, for us, I think the fun/misery balance has been heaped in favour of fun by the move to a motorboat.

We had some qualms about taking the plunge over to the 'dark side' because there can be a divide between the owners of sailboats and the owners of motorboats. Perhaps because *Thea* is such a classic design we have not found this to be the case, much to our relief.

I'm pretty sure that we've extended our cruising life by making the change now – before we were pushed! And it's certainly worth considering if you have a partner who is a nervous/unwilling sailor – they may well be willing to spend more time afloat…

Last but not least

Finally, I think we'd like to thank each other… once again Team Owen, albeit a slightly creakier version than the one that built *Early Mist* and *Selene*, rose to the challenge. I am so grateful to Tom for his vision, skill and hard work, and I know he is grateful to me for my unwavering support and encouragement. Well done us!

Acknowledgements

We would like to express our sincere gratitude to the many companies who supplied us during our project. The following gave their professional help and advice throughout – their contribution and enthusiasm was invaluable:

- Premier Marinas and, in particular, the management and staff at Noss on Dart Marina
- Robbins Timber
- Beta Marine

Our thanks to Nick Burnham, Technical Contributor, *Motor Boat and Yachting Magazine* (*MBY*), who wrote an article for *MBY* about the building of *Thea* following her launch, and to the *MBY* Editor for granting us permission to use some of Nick's photographs.

Lightning Source UK Ltd.
Milton Keynes UK
UKHW051332061120
372565UK00005B/30